AF574392

FRONT & CENTER

HOW I LEARNED TO LIVE THERE

Amnesia of the past, a work in progress
Disengage the weakening mirror
Cradle the optic mind

Release the ocean

Shower your shoulders with strength
Increase your connection to the magnificent
Affect your potential with honor

Embrace this walk, Front and Center

Carlton Wilborn

Front & Center

How I Learned To Live There

I would really like to hear from you. Please share your comments by sending them to the email address below. Thank you so much.

FRONT & CENTER
A Treelife Publishing Book

P.O. Box 480462
Los Angeles, California 90048
carlton@treelifepublishing.com
www.treelifepublishing.com

Edited by Vivien Cooper
Book Design by Emiko North
Photography by Linda Posnick
Back cover photo by Michael Higgins

Printed by Lightning Source International
Distributed by Ingram and Baker & Taylor

First Edition
Manufactured in the United States of America

ISBN 978-0-9790052-1-3

LCCN 2006910090

Contents

Contents

Contents

ACKNOWLEDGEMENTS

All the while in this process it was clear to me that I needed to give a wholehearted thank you to God, my Lord and savior. God, without your love and your guidance, there is no way this book would have ever come into such a powerful and beautiful form. I also give a wide open thank you to both my mother and my father, and my entire Windy City tribe, for giving me that blank canvas to create my own path of identity. And of course I give a big hug of thanks to my editor, Vivien Kooper. Vivien, your proficiency of editing, shaping, and bringing more punch to this book, as well as your ways of holding my soul during the trying days, have proven to be truly the work of an angel. Then there's Emiko North – a big ups to you for your joy and relentless dedication to designing my book with such elegance, power and polish. To all my friends that I mention in this book, as well as the ones near and far, that have shown me that you really care – you know who you are – a large shout out of thanks. To my Big Apple soulmate, Andrea Cooper, I give a special thank you, for believing in me from the get-go. To Pauline Nash, my life coach, you know the role you've played in making this dream come true. This is only the beginning. Thank you so very much. And where would I be if it were not for all of you out there, who entered my life for a season, and the reason, of causing me to stretch. You're the ones that really carved the journey for this book.

This Book is Dedicated to
All the Broken Kites

Blowing in the wind, designed to fly high
Held by a cord of strength

This Is the Kite

Brother Bobie was established for the same
But his wings became broken and so they allowed for no
rainbow destination

His heart so ornamented with sorrow
Offered no sunroof freedom for his season
He seemed to miss the ball for the slam-dunk of luck
And he longed for the freshness of the fall
to place him in Zion
But to his dismay no locksmith arrived
To unhitch his halloweened reality

Bobie was The Broken Kite

Because he allowed his mental garden of figs and berries
To be decorated by people who never even learned
To clean their own fortress
Bobie became much blinded by their rebuking

And regret and self-doubt captured his soul

Though all kites must be protected from the storm
Bobie never seemed to find that cushion of rescue
linked to the Majestic Master in Command

And because of IT he remained riddled and broken

May your heart rest in peace now, Brother
Augustus Wilborn Jr: aka Bobie

The Broken Kite

INTRODUCTION

Over the years, I have said to several close friends that getting this book finished and out to the public was going to be *the most courageous thing I would ever do.*

The journey began in the fall of 2001. I had really hit rock bottom in my career as a dancer and actor, and I was a few months behind on my rent. I was forced to move out of my townhouse apartment in order to avoid having my landlord follow through with evicting me. I searched and searched for solutions that would remedy my dizzying situation. I even thought of quitting the whole entertainment business and running home – as if moving back would truly cure what had gotten me into such a pickle of misfortune. It became a quick-fix idea for me. But *that,* my soul knew, was not the honest answer to my problem.

Then two things rose up in me. First was the decision that I was not going to move back to Chicago. No, I decided, that choice would have been way too cowardly for me. And it would have created the subtext that Los Angeles and its entertainment machine had actually won the battle, reducing my life to a full buffet of failures. And that version of reality I just would not accept.

Secondly, I had to admit that it was me who had gotten me into the position I was in, and that it was going to be up to *me* to restore and then rebuild all that had been destroyed.

At least I still had some solid friends to lean into, and so I did, gratefully. And it was while living in my first temporary home space, with my friend Myron, that the seed for this tell-all journey began to sprout. It started with a decision that I had to make myself be very productive during that frigid time. Somewhere deep inside of me, I knew that all that dread was going to have to come to an end at some point. And when it did, I had to be able to smile, knowing that at least I had taken my life forward in some fashion.

I decided I would begin my climb out of my pit by facing my past through writing poetry. That rescue mission quickly began demanding more and more of a commitment from me, and it was that process that became the initial salve for the wound of humiliation which had taken a pillar position in my heart.

The title of my book, "Front & Center," was chosen as a metaphor for *standing up*… Standing up to guilt, fear, and shame, all brought about by the mental prisons I let myself be trapped inside of, by identifying myself in limiting ways – as a victim of child abuse, as a sex addict, as a drug abuser, as someone suffering from physical challenges and low self-esteem. I've come to realize that happened for no other reason than for me to condition my mind with perseverance, learn the truth about myself, increase my faith, and then stand up with a testimony to serve all those still living in hiding for *whatever unnecessary reasons.* I cannot deny that while writing, I was facing wobbly knees over the reality that all of this personal information would be finally exposed; especially at the risk of forfeiting my dream of that powerful career as an entertainer. It is the career I hoped would make *me* powerful.

All my life, I have admired those fierce warrior-type beings throughout existence, those who have lived their lives radically so as to assist in creating more freedom for a larger humanity. This book is my tribute and my contribution to their works. So even as I stand, with a nervous center, I know that this work will far surpass the power I had given to any movie or TV role I could ever acquire.

May we all release ourselves from that war zone in our minds that keeps us forever held hostage and paralyzed against progress. I deliver this book finally from the *incarnation of my most powerful self.* And I do it for all of us FRONT AND CENTER.

FREE

Dance Dance Dance, this is what they'd say
They Him Her... Enough Already!

When did what I thought
become so insignificant to me?

Freedom is what I suppose I was after
the way for my freedom I just would not let be
or I hope the truth is that I just could not see

So many victories yet so many doubts
I can be many things Have been so many things
But what am I supposed to be?

Oh here they come, "The You Should Battalion"
Her Them and Him, ready to beat me down
if I don't say Yes
Yes to everything they want to see
Ain't it time for me becoming me

You see... I was born a Gemini and anybody
that's ever come close to that piece of the Heavenly Puzzle
knows that I As Me am a vast museum in and of myself

Intriguing Sometimes Dark Sometimes Beautiful
Confusing Inspiring Seriously Sincere and Surely
Sometimes Shallow

But that's only truly IF you choose to
open your delivery station and ever so lovingly
pack me in a box to be shipped to the land of
many declarations with
no solutions
In the mirror there it is

The Peace The Fear The Cold
The Child There it is… The Aggressive and The Passive
versions of me Thank You very much…

I been livin' life y'all, so call me what you may
But don't get it twisted…
I've only just begun to truly becoming me
the Me that GOD established
The me that you will see this time around as
FREE REALLY FREE

So yes… I'll accept their invitation… I Will Dance
But you better sit back and stay tuned cause this time
I'm dancin'… and dancin'… and dancin' my life
just like Missy Elliot and Mr. Mozart

Surprising Grace

"*You are amazing! Wow! I just want to help you.*" These were the kind of statements poured onto me in the summer of 2005 while working in San Juan, Puerto Rico. From one single phone call, I was placed in what I can only define as The Most Anointed Time of My Life.

I received a phone call from the actress Roselyn Sanchez, wanting me to choreograph a feature film she was starring in, entitled *Yellow.* Roselyn is a longtime friend of mine – we had met about eight years earlier. She is also a producer, and was the developer of the movie. More importantly, she was *the angel* chosen to place me in a cocoon of everlasting bliss. As excited as I was to get her call, I must tell you that I was also seriously taken aback because it came at a time when I was honestly in the belief that Roselyn had written me off as a friend after an especially dark period in my life.

Nevertheless, this would go down as *the experience* that anchored me deeply in the rich knowledge that *God was and always has been working for me, and working for me full steam ahead.* This was a time for me of receiving favor upon favor. This was my moment of Surprising Grace. Let's get into it.

Before my 2005 communication with Roselyn, the last time we really connected, I was in a dark "well period" in my life. This is a phrase I recently heard coined by Iyanla Vanzant, speaker, author of many profound books, and star of the hit TV show "Starting Over." Iyanla uses that phrase to describe those times in our lives when we suddenly realize we've either fallen into, dug ourselves into, or been put into, *a dark well* – figuratively speaking, of course. And there we are – *in the well* – not sure how we got there, what it all means, or how to get out.

My "Well Period" took place somewhere around 2001, after I returned from having a very unpleasant experience working on a cruise ship. The ship situation was wrong, *so wrong*, mainly because it was structured in a way that was literally designed for the employees to think extremely small of themselves – and my ego wanted no part of that insanity. There I was, chosen to be a leader, the Dance Captain on the ship, overseeing ten to twelve other performers – something I had never before been set up to do – as well as working my butt off performing two shows a day, six days a week, only to have the ship's director say straight to our faces, "You don't matter at all." He was not mincing words. "You don't matter at all. It's only about the passengers." That version of negative acknowledgment was completely unacceptable to me.

That was layered with the fact that we were also told, "You are not allowed to eat in the area where the better food is." They tried to sanction us to the musty, smelly, second-fiddle kitchen area – us, the performers, the people responsible for not only bringing the patrons a great experience, but also bringing the ship a greater reputation. How twisted is that? All of that craziness almost caused me to fall emotions-first into my old Chicago self, and open up a serious can of "whoop-ass."

I never did actually roll up my sleeves and settle into laying blows all over that man's head. But I did get myself into many crazy screaming matches with him, started lashing out at the other dancers, and even found myself strutting around my really ugly ego attitude, all just to make the statement that I would, by no stretch of the imagination, be taken advantage of.

Oh yeah, I was for sure in "the well," and all sides of it were grimy and slimy. But, being the person I am, I also knew I couldn't just abandon something because it was hard. No, that's not how I'm built. I knew I had to go in deep, and find some degree of faith in God, some faith that He had worked this out exactly as it was, to be in some way a benefit for me. So I unclenched my fists, let go of all thoughts of hunting for an escape ladder, and stuck it out 'til the end of my six month contract. It didn't feel great, but

I had to do what I had to do.

Anyway, continuing with the Roselyn thing, and me being back in Los Angeles, I returned home from the ship with the intention to make my life feel a hell of a lot better than that traveling-the-seas excursion. To my shock and surprise, even after a solid nine months of being home, I found I could not land a single job to save my life – no pun intended.

Had being dealt with in such degrading ways actually rubbed off on me and made me truly inadequate? I was praying that wasn't the case, but I really wasn't sure, because this was *the darkest* my life had ever become. I was battling some strange allergy syndrome – asthma, weight loss, and sinus congestion. I was feeling so bad, I didn't even want to eat the best homemade meatloaf or sweet potato pie. It was all too much, and I began feeling really suicidal.

The thought, "What the fuck is going on?" just kept racing through me. Yes, I suppose I had fallen into a heavy depression, and yes, I was feeling fear like never before. And this sure was not the version of my life I had intended to build. I kept feeling like I should have been able to shake it off much faster than what was happening. I didn't really know what was going on, but I was clear it wasn't good.

I was aware that deep within that lonely, cavernous well, Faith had to be out there floating around somewhere. I was just having a seriously hard time grabbing hold of it.

Now, at the time of my downfall, Roselyn's acting career was blowing up in a fabulous way. Having been in the industry for well over fifteen years at the time myself, I also knew that what she was involved in required very intense focus, so she could not be burdened down with my oozing, muddy stuff. And being the kind of artist that she is, I knew she wouldn't let herself be, either. I know that sounds kind of harsh, but that is the way the cookie crumbles in Hollywood. Now let's jump forward.

Somewhere around 2003, with my life still in a bit of a pit, I reached out to my friend again, this time to ask for a much-needed loan of fifteen hundred dollars (which I was later able to repay, thanks to the Puerto Rico experience). I thought it best if we meet at her place for the exchange. There was no way I'd have egg on my face by having her find out I was now in the single room space I was forced to move into. Then again, I also had no idea she was now living in a million dollar home. That staggering reality only caused my tail, which was already tucked far under my ass, to curve even further under.

All that tail-tucking turned out to be unnecessary because like a good, true friend, she stepped eagerly forward. She handed over the funds without ever batting an eye – I'm sure partly because, though I am a good actor and all, capable of many transformations, the sadness I was so desperately trying to disguise was something she could smell all over me. Nevertheless, I gladly took her gift, squirmed myself home as quickly as I could, and prayed for the best. That was pretty much the most communication she and I had that year.

Cut to 2005. For some reason, early that year, I began thinking about Roselyn all the time. Any time I went near a magazine stand, I searched to see if her face would appear glowing glamorously off the pages. This went on for months and months, but never did I find her staring back at me from the multitude of paper stacks. It sounds a bit stalker-like, but that was not the case. I was just really missing my friend.

Now, by this point in my life, things were definitely on the up slope, but never could I have imagined that during those very demeaning "well" days, God was building in me a seed of focus that would pay off so big – and man, did it ever.

The time I spent in Puerto Rico on the movie turned out to be a solid two months, and involved weekly director/production meetings, location scouting, and the responsibility for, and opportunity to, cast and choreograph over forty performers who performed over six different scenes, designed from four different styles of movement – ballet, hip hop, contemporary, and flamenco. My time there was also much about the locals sugaring me up ever so sweetly – whether I was going to Walgreen's or just strolling to bask in the electrifying sun – and about the half dozen interviews I was set up to do.

All of this was so powerful for me, I just knew it had to be about *God…God – in relation to my degree of Faith.* I tell you, there was gratitude flowing through me like I had never experienced before.

The time I spent working with Roselyn was absolutely fantastic. For the first five weeks, we would start together around 10:30 in the morning with a ballet class for one hour, we'd take an hour lunch, and then get into rehearsing for nearly three hours, finishing the day around 3:30 p.m., sometimes even later. Whatever time I finished, it still allowed me to bask in that forever healing, crystalline Atlantic Ocean. I felt like I was being baptized every single time I went in the water. Without question, that was, as my good friend Niki says, A Good Life Moment.

Roselyn was so great to me, she really made sure that I was kept in the loop about everything that was going on, from the changes with the directors, to producer issues, and even down to the crazy emailing that was floating back and forth. Best of all, she allowed me to go all out with whatever I wanted to do creatively. No artist could ever ask for anything more. Especially when you're being paid so well on top of it.

Had my Faith meditations for deliverance, those meditations during my dark "well" times, produced this grandiose shower of blessings? I can only think, yes! But the most curious thing about that whole journey was how so many of the frustrating elements I was forced to be involved in on that cruise ship later revealed themselves to me as God-ordained circumstances designed to be early schooling tools.

I could now see that everything on the cruise ship had unfolded the way it had in order to prepare me for a proper leadership position. Everything that happened was designed to help me see how far I needed to fine-tune my character so as to be a better manager of other people when put in a position of much responsibility.

What I am getting better at accepting is that, through it all, during the "well" times, if we can work *even harder* with ourselves to hang on to even the dullest degree of faith, we will eventually arrive at a much more gratifying reality. It might be hard, but we can make it through. Who's to say? Our newfound Faith might even produce continuous Surprising Grace.

"'Dude, it's time to actually connect with your family. You need to go deal with your Dad.'

Those words were echoing inside as I returned from that blessed time in Puerto Rico in the summer of 2005. God had really been showing out for me, and it was making me realize I needed to stop my bullshit – and me pretending I didn't need a major relationship with my dad was part of my bullshit.

Growing up, I had so many issues for so many years as to what was wrong with my family, and I had put it on my Dad as the one responsible for the chaos. So, my Dad and I didn't really have a close relationship. Going to visit him would be a big-deal trip for me – the first time that as grown, adult men, we would have some real time to just hang out together. I was a bit nervous about it.

Anyway, with my inner voice leading me, I was about to find myself visiting Augusta,

Georgia right after Thanksgiving of that same year…"

GEORGENE'S GIFT

"By the time I was ready to move out of our house and go out on my own, my Dad was half beat up, his health was funky, and he was driving an old raggedy station wagon.

Later, after my Mom passed away, he felt called to go back home to Georgia. I couldn't believe he actually did it – went back home and started over. He moved back to Augusta, bought a brand new house, bought a brand new car, and even made a whole new connection with a woman.

I knew it was a huge thing for a man his age to make a major change like that, and I

could tell it was just the comfort zone that he needed. Obviously, our family environment was so bad for him that it had every area of his life falling apart. Then, when he got away from us, he was able to put it all back together.

When I got to my Dad's house, he was with Rosa, his new lady. I didn't recognize her but she remembered me from when I was a kid and I used to stay with my Aunt Rose and my Aunt Georgene in Florida during the summers..."

The year was 1978 and I was a freshman in high school. I had just come off some turbulent school days – too many fights, several suspensions – and my parents knew it was time for a change. I needed a break. Something different.

I thought and I thought about where I might want to go. I decided to go live with Aunt Rose, my father's sister who had set up shop in Florida. I intended to stay there through the entire four years of high school – plans which were quickly thwarted. You see, Aunt Rose had plans of her own. She was under the impression I was there to be her servant. And she kept me on lockdown for hours throughout the day like some kind of juvenile delinquent.

I quickly developed a very strong desire to leave Florida, but the truth be told, Aunt Rose was only part of the problem. My need to leave the state surfaced when Aunt Rose's sister took things a little too far in the area of discipline. Here's the deal. Aunt Rose and Aunt Georgene lived down the street from each other, and spent most of their time at Aunt Rose's house. I had gone to stay over at Aunt Georgene's place for a couple of days. I had been looking forward to going because I really liked her. She made me laugh a lot, and she could cook her butt off.

Now, while I was at her house, I chose to make two – that's two – phone calls to my family back in Chicago. I remember us having nice conversations, nothing crazy. And I remember that we didn't talk for that long. I had simply felt a need to speak to my family, my parents to be exact, and I didn't see anything wrong with that. I didn't see anything wrong with it at all.

The first I heard of any reaction to my calling home was a few weeks later when I got a telephone call from Aunt Rose. She was calling from work to tell me that Aunt Georgene was upset with me for running up her phone bill, and she warned me that when Aunt Georgene got home from work that day, I was going to be in a lot of trouble.

I was thinking, "Huh? I ran up her phone bill? How had I done that?" I knew I had made a couple of calls, but I was having trouble putting together the brevity of those calls I'd made and the intensity of her voice. Her tone let me know that in Aunt Georgene's mind, the couple of phone calls had become a much larger issue than they were in my mind.

It was around 2:30 in the afternoon when that call came in. Now, when I say that the three hours between 2:30 p.m. and 5:30 p.m., when she and Aunt Georgene were due home from work, were some of the longest three hours I'd ever experienced, you'd better believe I'm telling the truth. I couldn't watch TV, I couldn't relax and enjoy the sounds of my favorite radio station, and I was surely in no state of mind to study. The message I'd been given was that once that door opened and Aunt Georgene was standing in the doorway, the proverbial shit was going to hit the fan. And I had gotten the message loud and clear.

The hours passed by so slowly it was excruciating. Later, I was in the front yard burning some weeds off the surrounding fence with gasoline. Or maybe I had just finished cleaning up Aunt Rose's home beauty salon, or picking ticks off her dogs – just a few of the many servant duties that were assigned to me to justify my presence at Aunt Rose's. I don't remember which task I was engaged in at the time, but what I do know for sure is that when I looked up, all I could see was Aunt Georgene's car coming down the block, swerving through all the children playing in the street. She drove as if she were being chased by murderers.

She zoomed that car forward so fast that she didn't even take the time to get it neatly parked in the driveway before she jumped out and started rushing towards me, cursing. Believe me, this wasn't the first time in my life I had experienced the anger of a guardian, but this was different. She was truly coming at me not just to reprimand me but to kick my ass. Now, being a young boy of fourteen, and having grown up on the wild streets of Chicago, I knew that when somebody came up on you looking that twisted out, the only thing to do was to get busy runnin', so that's exactly, without question, what I did.

I ran straight for the house. I made it inside the front door, but just as I went to slam the door closed, Mrs. Kick-My-Ass was hot on my heels. I darted to the left, snatched myself to the right, and headed down the hall towards the bathroom. Now, all I was thinking was "get in that little room and lock the door quickly," but Aunt Georgene was faster than I was. Before I could shut her out, she had her arm stuck in the door, and she forced her way inside. Unfortunately, she got to lock the door with me inside, and the scene turned darker and darker as the seconds rolled along.

She proceeded to yell at me, saying that all of this was because of the $17.00 – which for her was completely unheard of – that I had run up on her phone bill by calling home to Chicago. In my haste to lose her when I bolted into the house, I guess I missed the fact that she had somehow managed to get an extension cord into her hands. I'm talking about that common brown electrical cord, made of rubber or plastic or whatever.

Anyway, she had that thing wrapped up in her hands and she proceeded to go at me with it, using serious force. She swung and she swung. I tried to block as many hits as possible, but between her screaming and her flailing arms, she was getting the best of me. I don't know how long it lasted, but I do know that by the time she stopped, she was sweating pretty seriously. And as for me, I was left with clearly visible, open wounds on my body. My arms, legs, and back were *gashed*. I'm not talking about uncomfortable welts here. I'm talking full-on blood flowin'. She meant business, and her business, her damage, was done.

She won. She won... And I was furious. And humiliated. I mean, I was the spoiled youngest son of my family, and I had never in my entire life been hit like that. *And I mean never.* It was then and there that I knew that the whole bullshit Florida arrangement was going to come to a screeching halt, and not a moment too soon.

That night, I got on the phone to Chicago, and this time, I didn't give a fuck how long I talked. I wanted my parents to know exactly how I was being treated. I knew there was no way they would have any part in that kind of insanity. Within minutes of getting on the phone with me, my parents were pissed, and I mean *fire-red* pissed. My mom started crying and my dad – well, I had never heard him like that. He was outraged. It was all perfect. Perfect. They did exactly what I needed them to do to rescue me from that disgusting reality.

All it took was that one phone call. My dad told me I could come home whenever I wanted, asked me when I wanted to come home, and never asked another question. Of course, I said I wanted to go home right away, and he honored my request. He never asked to speak to either Aunt Rose or Aunt Georgene. I hung up the phone with the strongest "I dare you to touch me again" look on my face, and it was a done deal. I was on my way out. The end of my Florida school days came three days later. I had a plane ticket in my hand and I was going home. That was the end of that, but it was also the beginning – the beginning of what was to become my very special life.

When I made it home, we had to make a move, and fast. I had left Florida in the middle of the school year and my parents didn't want to waste any time in getting me placed somewhere else. My mom had a brilliant thought and decided to call my eighth grade teacher. They had shared some good conversations when they ran into each other in the grocery store, so my mom felt safe calling her. Her name was Carolyn Currie, and she had been very fond of me before I graduated from grammar school.

It worked. Carolyn said she knew someone that worked at Whitney Young Magnet High School, and she thought they might be able to help me. Normally, in order to be accepted into the school, I would have had to have passed some major academic tests earlier in the year. Unfortunately, we had already missed that deadline period. After some brainstorming, Carolyn came up with something fantastic. She was going to introduce me to Diane Brooks, her colleague at Whitney Young who worked as the head of the dance department. She was sure Diane could help me, so I met with her and within seconds, she took a fancy to me, and said she could make it happen.

The plan she devised to get me into the school required me to audition through the dance department come September. She offered to step up and work with me as a coach, helping me perfect my routine over the summer, so that when September came around, I would pass the audition and get into the dance program. My mom and Carolyn really wanted this to happen because at the time, Whitney

Young was the third top public school in the nation.

Well, we got on it. We rehearsed and rehearsed for weeks, and by the time the end of August rolled around, my audition piece was complete and my audition time was set. When September arrived, the whole audition process flowed like a perfect autumn day. I showed up on time wearing my makeshift dance outfit – t-shirt, sweat pants, new K-Swiss gym sneakers. My hair was perfectly groomed, all shiny and in a perfectly trimmed afro. Sitting squarely around my shoulders was my new, freshly bought backpack/dance bag. I was ready to go.

I was taken by myself into a room, and they asked me what I was going to do. I plopped some song into a boom box – I don't even remember what it was – and proceeded to do my thing. I don't actually recall much of that day at all, other than the memory of Diane sitting there with the other adjudicators, wishing me well and holding our little secret. As if we were strangers. As if we had never met. To this day, I'm not sure what made Diane so willing to help us. I'll never know why she said "Yes." I mean, she had never gotten to see me do any movement of any kind before agreeing to the whole thing.

A week later, Carolyn called to say I was accepted. Our plan had worked. I was entering the arts department at Whitney Young, where I would train to become a dancer. The whole experience, beginning with what went down in Florida, was really the beginning of me learning to honor myself. At the time, I did not have a heightened awareness of the impact of the choice I was making. I was brought up to speed some twenty-seven years later when I was awakened to the realization that my entire geographic transfer, and everything that lead up to my transfer out of Florida, was actually a divine plan to get me to Hollywood.

The reasons I did it, the way I did it, and the timing of it all – everything was guided so that I could arrive at my life in entertainment. It is a life that continually broadens me, and blesses me every day. And for that, I guess I must say "Thank you, Aunt Georgene. You set me free." The mysterious curves of life surely can be awesome teachers themselves, if we will only let them be.

"It was awesome getting to see my Dad. The day I arrived, his girlfriend Rosa seemed to instinctively know that my Dad and I needed some time, so after little introductions, she left us alone.

He has always been into gardening, and he walked me through his new garden, showing me all the different kinds of veggies, pointing out which ones were about to sprout, showing it all off to me – collard greens, turnips, tomatoes, watermelon. We must have sat together for two and a half hours out by his little garden patch, and it was so great to finally have that kind of time with him.

As my Dad and I sat there sharing with each other, Gary's name came up. Gary was a

friend of the family, and the son of my Aunt Rose's old boyfriend.

Dad had no idea at all what the name Gary meant to me. There I was, truly getting to visit with my Dad for the first time, and I had this huge area of my life that he knew nothing about.

In my mind, my trip to visit my Dad had been all about his mortality. He was getting older, and I was thinking, 'You've got to go and do this now.' I was thinking I'd been led there for no other reason than the fact that I didn't want to wake up one day, discover that my Dad was gone, and realize I had never reached out to him. It never even occurred to me to bring up the subject of Gary – but Gary stuff kept surfacing.

As my Dad and I were hanging out together by his garden, and Gary's name came up a couple of times, finally I realized I was being guided by Spirit to talk to my Dad about what had happened.

So later, when he was driving me around his old neighborhood, showing me where he grew up, and pointing out all the areas that were meaningful to him, I said, 'Dad, at some point I want to talk to you about Gary."

We rode around together, and it was phenomenal. He drove past his old grammar school and his high school. He showed me where he started fishing. He drove me past the old, little bitty house where he grew up. Looking at the steps of that house, and listening to Dad talk about his best friends, I could see him as a little kid running up and down the steps of that house. The whole thing was huge.

Leaving the neighborhood my Dad had grown up in, I started feeling all tick-tock inside. We were driving to Blockbuster to get some movies to watch later, and my inner voice started saying to me, 'Dude, are you going to do it now? You better do it now…'

We pulled into the parking lot of Blockbuster and I said to my Dad, 'I want to talk to you now about Gary. There's stuff I've wanted to tell you, Dad.'

'Uh-huh,' he said.

'It's been a long time, Dad, way overdue, but I need to tell you… I was sexually molested by Gary when I was a kid.'

He said nothing, just kept looking straight ahead. He seemed to be trying to digest what I was telling him.

'It happened in Florida during the years when I was eight years old until I was thirteen. And it's been a really crazy thing for me.'

'Oh, Lord, Carl. Damn, Carl…' My dad started moaning, 'Ah, Carl, oh Lord… I don't know what to say now.'

I continued, 'It's been a really hard thing for me in all these different areas of my life – my sexuality, my diagnosis – I've been so confused… Anyway, Dad, that's what happened.'

Then my Dad finally broke, saying 'I always knew something was up with that damned man. Then he had all that stuff go down with him and those other boys.'

'Other boys? What other boys?'

'Your Aunt Rose told me he got arrested and went to jail for that shit,' he said.

I knew that he had gotten turned in by one other little boy when I was sixteen years old. I remember very well standing in the kitchen when my Mom got the phone call from my Aunt Rose. It was a moment I would never forget.

I was looking at my Mom and she was looking at me.

'Rose just told me,' my Mom said to me, 'that Gary just lost his job because some boy turned him in for sexual molestation.'

My Mom was looking right at me and I was petrified. 'I know that wouldn't happen to you,' she said, 'because you're smarter than

that.'

My Mom's statement to me that day was the thing that made it so hard for me to be in my truth..."

My Helpful Cloud

"She knew 'that would never happen to me.' Because I was smarter than 'that.' I was mortified, but I didn't say anything. I just looked at my Mom – like Ice Boy. As a kid, my entire home environment was really heavy. Between my Dad being an alcoholic, and him beating up my Mom and my older brother, Bobie, I learned to be guarded. Then you add into that mix the things I would hear from my Mom about my Dad cheating, and the fact that I knew my Mom was also cheating – and I was nervous about all of it. Havin' all that up on me is what turned me into Ice Boy.

I used to tell myself, 'You can't be too soft, or you won't withstand all this pressure.' Little did I know how much pressure I'd really have to deal with later on in my life."

It was mid-February of 1985 in Hawaii – Oahu to be exact. I had never been there, so to some degree I was thrilled – on the surface, anyway. Inside, I was feeling pretty tight. The tightness was there because all the cards had not yet been put on the table for me.

I remember it vividly... standing in front of the side table next to my bed, feeling the solemn mood that was created in the entire room by the fact that the overhead lights had been turned off. The bed was folded down perfectly, thanks to the maid that came along while I was out for breakfast. There was that flaccid color of beige everywhere I turned... the painted walls, the blankets, the pillows, the carpet. Even the telephone in my hand was matching that vacant-of-life color scheme.

So, anyway, I'm holding that telephone, knowing I need to start dialing, but it is like I am in some bad TV phone moment where, over and over again, the character you're watching starts to dial but keeps stopping. Then they dramatically slam down the phone in utter frustration. Only, the sad reality for me was that *I was not watching the tube.* I was in a real life reality moment with myself. Finally, unlike the person on TV, I eventually found my strength and made the call.

The phone begins to ring, and I am praying that I can

hold steady and maintain my composure. Then, the other end picks up and I speak. "Hi, this is Carlton Wilborn. Is doctor so-and-so in?" The receptionist says "Yes, hold please." Now, at this point, I'm thinking "If she makes me hold too long, I'm not waitin', I'm gonna hang this phone up." But within seconds, the doctor's voice chimes in, and he says "Hi, is this Carlton?" I say "Yes," and he tries to start some small talk about how I'm enjoying Hawaii and all that, but I think he can hear the curtness in my tone of voice so he moves right in to address what I am calling about.

At this point, he says *"Are you sitting down?"* Now, I'm not stupid. I know that kind of intro is no set-up for good news. *Then he says "The test we did came back and you are HIV positive."*

In that second, I mentally left the room. I don't know where I went exactly, but I was clearly void of hearing anything the doctor was talking about. All I remember was feeling my right eyebrow raised up stark-high on my forehead – that's what happens when I get real serious about something. My arms, I remember, were crossed under the phone across my chest, as if they had their own mind and were trying to hold me up and keep me from falling pathetically to the floor. My heart began beating so loud and hard, it was as if it was in my throat, trying to stop me from breathing.

I felt like I was underneath some very strange cloud that had urgently rolled in, gloating at me as I went from absolute fear to being angry, to quickly turning into some scared, human-like turtle, hiding inside myself. Suddenly, the sound of the doctor was back. He was saying something about me needing to see him when I got back home, and telling me that there were some drugs he thought "might" help. *Yes, you heard me. He said "I think they might help." There was no assurance for my safety in his voice at all.* I tried to listen on, and then quietly, I said "Okay" and hung up the phone.

I don't think I moved from that spot for at least a few minutes. I had to hold myself steady, and really take in what had just been dropped on me. Then, I grabbed my already packed dance bag and proceeded out of the room, down the hall, through the hotel, and onto the bus for the theater. I had to go to that lovely tech rehearsal for the shows we were in sunny Hawaii to do. All of this I mustered up in total freak-out mode because that strange cloud rolled in. But my freak-out was being hidden behind my trying-not-to-crumble facade.

That single phone call forever changed how I would think about beautiful Hawaii; and set me off on the journey to really know myself. *My truth.*

Once we were all in the theater, everyone made their way to the stage to begin what is always a grueling process of stop and start, to set the lighting and finalize who should stand perfectly where. I was not needed for the first few numbers, so instead of sitting privately in my dressing room feeling sorry for myself, I chose to sit out in the house and face all that was upon me head-on. I sat staring at all the dancers on that stage, doing all the challenging things we as dancers in a company have to do. Watching them helped me stay connected to the force of strength that I had to accept was not just *around* me, but *inside* me. This would be the building block strategy for dealing with my glooming news.

The day carried on, and so did the tour. Nothing seemed to be that significant to me. We danced, there was applause, there were flowers, and there were after parties with many compliments from the adoring fans – but none of it registered really. I just kept thinking about what I had to face when I got back home, because while yes, I had received that "real" information from the doctor, I was *just on tour*, and when you're on tour, whatever goes on there is not really *reality*. Reality only truly kicks in once you are back at home on your own turf.

My next real focused moment regarding what I would later begin to think of as My Helpful Cloud happened when I was back in Chicago. I was at the dance studio, which was downtown with not much surrounding it but the L tracks to protect if from being hit by The Hulk – the local term for the harsh wind. Man, it was freezing outside, so the windows were all fogged out. It was just before 10:00 in the morning, we were getting ready to take company class, and at that hour the studio wasn't even close to being warm yet. So, I was dressed in layers of a t-shirt, sweatshirt, long john underwear instead of tights, and I had leg warmers up over my knees as well, with a scarf thrown around my neck. Yes, this was my normal attire at that time of year, but now I was much more concerned about it. I was taking no chances with catching a cold or anything like that, especially not with the secret information I now had.

So, there I was, doing my warm-up, watching the other dancers come in. I suppose I was cordial to them to some degree, but I was much more focused on my attitude. Inside, I was feeling as cold as that winter day. The cloud that had rolled in turned me into an even harder person than my abusive past had already stirred up. I was watching me from outside myself, and the expression I could see on my face was that of the new version of warrior that had taken residence in my soul.

I was doing some pliés and stretching exercises, and I was absolutely clear in that exact moment that this "cloud thing," this at-that-time-thought-to-be death sentence, *was in no way going to win over me.* That, as Oprah would say, was surely a "defining moment" for me. Oh yes, I had heard what the diagnosis was, but on that cold winter day, fully tuned into my body, I had defiantly decided, that *this crazy "killer disease" was in no way going to take me out.* That headstrong side of me that handled the Southside streets of Chicago kicked into full gear, and that ballet class that day was one of the best I remember ever having.

I have to say that, while this whole health thing has been cumbersome, and confusing sometimes, it has also, without question, guided me to become more ferocious in my understanding of *exactly who and what I truly am.* Not the "I am" based on what other people decide, but the "I am" based on my most divine identity.

Did I fall into a period of depression regarding my chilling Hawaii news? *Yes, I did.* But, one thing I've been learning over the years is that most things existing in our lives, from material things, to people, to even our seem-to-be-ruling-over-us thoughts, are there because somewhere in a quiet pocket of our physical structure *we have given the thing permission to be there*, to take full residence in our soul and rest there with complete assurance that we are its absolutely, perfectly established, should-be home.

This, I now understand, is not what living is all about. We are not here to be mere caverns, where anything that wants to slum around in us can do so. We are not Bounty Paper Towels designed to suck up anything that is placed in front of us. I remember so vividly something a past lover said to me once at the beginning of our relationship. We were at his house discussing our connection, and he was expressing how he was into it, and the fact that he had no apprehensions about it. "Yes," he admits, "I have met people and started things out all hot-and-heavy and then been severely burned." I quickly jump in and say "Well then, how can you just say that you can trust so easily?" And, without a beat, he says "Because I choose to."

Mister Rodney M., the man that had entered my life and was slowly melting my ice-blocked heart said, "It's a choice… you decide to do it, or not do it, then you stand by your choice." I looked at him with utter amazement and respect, and in that moment, I realized that this way of thinking was what had kept me alive and healthy throughout all those years.

Yes, my moment in that cold Chicago studio was my

moment of absolute decision. There is a powerful prophetic tape that I've had since the fall of 2001. It speaks about the course of events in mental evolution over a twelve year span from 2000 to 2012, where we are growing into the Kings and Queens we once were, who were able to do miraculous things, like control weather and build pyramids without state-of-the-art equipment, as the Egyptians once did. It's titled "Define, Focus and Create," and the activity of this title truly has been the foundation of how I am living my life today.

Yes, I would have to say the whole HIV thing, for me, has actually been the catalyst for my increased self-understanding and my increased faith. It has taught me how to love myself better, how to care for others more authentically, and where my real power stems from. Before I received that call, I was completely living my life self-consumed, in many ways that were seriously destructive. Getting my diagnosis made me look for more – not more of things, per se – but more of what is true, *divinely true.* And then rest in it.

For me, that is Spirit, that power source that is invisible to the searching eye, but, like the blowing wind, still clearly exists. This has now gripped my mind. God graced me with a character quality that keeps me as forever a student, and this forever seeking-ness thing about me found the spirit realm – not as some lofty intellectual concept, but as a tangible force that I indeed witness every day no matter which direction my head turns.

I have also learned that Spirit is something one can feel,

and when I say *feel*, I mean *feel*, at the core of your being. When I allow myself to get quiet enough inside, I can actually experience the absolute force of Spirit. Through my studies I now understand that Spirit is itself twenty-four/seven, in full activity every single second of the day, and there is nothing that can ever diminish its identity. Everything that exists, ever has, or ever will exist, is Spirit *first* and has Spirit's life force at the core of its being. When I remember this, I know that as long as I keep maintaining my focus on this part of life that I can't see, I will be okay, because I am Spirit first – all powerful and all knowing, always.

Deciding to focus my attention on Spirit in this way helps me create the life that I desire, and holds me not just steady from day to day, but keeps my life thriving with good as well. Whether it's a nice comment that comes to me from someone about my character, material support that I get for the affairs of my day, or the blessings that show up that keep me physically strong, I know that it is *all* because of what Spirit is, and my having faith in it. The truth about Spirit is what I am now standing by. This is where my faith lies, and as strange as it is, I do have to say that I found my faith because of My Helpful Cloud. Ain't life curious?

Ferocious Faith

There is a mighty companion
that can forever bless the heart
But only unwavering dedication
can bring it forth to do its part

This companion I call Ferocious Faith
keeps us holding strong
Dissolving the demons in our way
that wish to linger far too long

Ferocious faith is in you deep
Ferocious faith can calm your sleep
Ferocious faith can melt the fears
and Ferocious faith will dry all tears

How blessed we are to bare such a treasure
that can gift us true beyond bountiful measure

We need simply to remember
when worry arrives
threatening to pull us apart
Kindly smile with ferocious faith
and let it rear its rescue start

A Night Time Dedication

"'Carl, I know one thing we can do to make this right. Let's try to get some money out of him. I know he's got some. Gary should pay for what he did to you. He's a minister now, you know.'

My Dad was going on like that and all I could say was, 'Dad, I don't know where I'm at with everything. I really don't.'

All I knew was that I had just really wanted to tell him. And now he knew. Then he kept going on, saying 'Your Aunt Rose can tell you where he's living. If you get in touch with her, she can help you. I know if you contacted her, she'd be more than willing.' And I was just sitting there, boiling inside.

He kept talking about me finding Rose and I was thinking, 'Fuck, why won't he help me? When is someone going to step up and make this easy for me?' I never said it, but he must have seen it on my face because he immediately said, 'Carl, what? What do you want me to do? If you want me to help you, I'll do whatever.' And right then, I just lost it, crying. That's all I wanted was for someone to help me deal with this.

We got out of the car and went into Blockbuster. It was strange because our intention had been to go and pick up a movie that I was in, because his girlfriend's grandkids wanted so see some of the movies I'd done. After what we'd just discussed, I could only think to myself, 'What fucking movie can I get that's going to top what I just said to him?'

Back at the house that evening, we didn't speak of Gary again. When I was finally ready to leave to go back to the hotel to sleep, he walked me to the door and gave me a hug. I could feel that he was really tuning in, and wanting to let me know he was there for me. His focus felt really special.

I left and went back to the hotel. It all felt really heavy to me, and I hoped it wouldn't ruin my vacation. What kept running through my mind was 'Fucking Hell, this is not what I wanted this trip to be about.'

At 2:30 in the morning, Spirit woke me up.

It was clear to me by now that I was going to end up contacting Gary at some point. 'Oh my goodness,' I thought, 'I've got to pray on this.'

I got on my knees, and I was praying to God about the whole thing, asking, 'Give me guidance…'

As I was in the midst of that, it came to me that I needed to have a conversation with my Mom. I had never talked to her about what had happened with Gary. I had always held my Mom on such a pedestal. I never wanted to say anything that would make her feel bad or offend her. So this was an intense choice for me.

It seemed like a shame that she wasn't physically on earth to talk to anymore, but I knew I had a relationship with her in spirit, and that I could talk to her and tell her everything from that place.

As soon as I started the conversation with my Mom, I felt intensely emotional – more than I had let myself feel since she had passed. Before I knew what was happening, I found myself screaming at the top of my lungs. And

I couldn't have cared less if the other hotel guests heard me or not.

'Mom, what the fuck were you thinking? How in the hell could you have said what you said to me that day when I was sixteen? You knew that would never happen to me because I was too smart? Come on. You knew what Gary had done to me, and you didn't care.

'I was always your protector – holding phone numbers for you, hiding information about bank accounts – I always had your back. I spent years covering for you with your boyfriends, making sure I kept your secrets. But when I needed you to cover my back, where the hell were you? You weren't there for me. It makes no fucking sense. Here I was all this time thinking you loved me!'

By the time I finished my rant to my mother, I had a stream running down my face. No joke. I had been totally out of control, just crazy. It had been long overdue and I felt seriously relieved. I then opened my eyes, and at the edge of the bed where I was doin' my thing was left the largest puddle of tears, just about the size of a Frisbee. I then got off my knees, blew my nose, climbed back into bed, and fell back asleep.

When I woke up, I felt like my head was spinning. On the one hand, I was really re-

lieved, but at the same time, I was also really feeling like, 'Oh no, I hope I didn't take it too far with my Mom. I hope she's not upset with me. Sometimes I can be too dramatic. I hope I wasn't milkin' it.'"

Rose blossoms of yellow define the Springtime delight you ignite in me. You are not glitz and flash – you are winds of pure elegance. You are the channel by which I was chosen to have life. You are the Urban Sistah Lady that molded strength onto us five little bits from your bosom.

I'm looking at my mother. She is all neat and pulled together, and she is leaving the house where I was born. And for whatever reason, she is holding a young baby – about two years old – in her arms. Instantly, time begins to travel along very fast and then I begin to sense that she's left me. This feeling goes on for some time, and *this* just doesn't feel good.

Now I'm seeing my father. He's walking around our house. But then I see another version of him sitting down, very relaxed. Then, all of a sudden, I see him as he begins to turn invisible. All of this keeps changing so quickly.

As I watch myself pacing around the rooms of my house, I also notice that my brother, Tony, is all alone in a closet, taking a nap. He's dressed well in brown slacks, wearing nice socks and dress shoes. His legs are spread wide open as he sleeps on his back. The closet Tony is in is fully bright inside and it's all cleaned up and tidy. Things are perfectly organized. It just screams *Order. Order. Order.*

But the thought, "Where is Mom? Has something happened?" starts rolling through my mind. All of this feels so very curious to me. But it's the Mom stuff that has me so uncomfortable inside. I keep thinking, "I hope she didn't do it like this. I really hope she didn't."

I decide to call my oldest sister, Felecia (the family calls her Fe), to tell her what's going on. Before I do, I decide to look outside and check just one last time, to see if Mom might still be out there somewhere. And then the blessing arrives. Like a creeping frame-for-frame picture show, I see my sister, Fe, driving up, and my mom is actually inside the car with her. I become so excited. The car is packed with family – kids, adults, immediate and extended family. The car is a cherry red Volkswagen looking thing. As it pulls up, I notice more clearly that my mom is sitting in the far back seat, perfectly perched, staring through the window directly at me.

The feeling on my soul – that she came back, that she had not done it yet – was so huge for me. I quickly started crying.

Cut to my mother, now on a stage, singing. The stage is a space that is an extension of our house, and Mom is on it, looking simply amazing. Everyone is watching her perform. It's a truly beautiful moment.

"Yeah! She came back! Jonnye Mae Breckinridge is in her element. And she's up on that stage, doin' her thing." That's what was soaring through my head. The love that was emanating from her was like being enveloped by the spell of a mid-summer nap, underneath plum and citrus trees. She then crosses, stage left, stops at the front of the stage, and throws her head back. She hits a perfect note and before I know it, *Oh My God… she's passing out!*

In that split second, my mother's body crumbles to the floor. "Oh shit. She's dying," I'm thinking. This is the moment I did not want to have happen. Instantly, the entire room – all the voices, all the music, all of it – goes completely silent. Silence. Utter silence swells up all around us. Not a single sound. But then, just like the woman I know her to be, she springs right back up, fights to find her focus, and lickety-split, is fully revived and has risen again, as if touched by some magician or enchanter. She continues to wow the crowd. She is all strength, knowledge, and finesse. "My mother, Jonnye Mae, ain't goin' down easy… and I'm so glad for it."

Cut to me, in another room, in my family's house. The television is on. It's actually showing Mom's face on the screen. The network news is doing a cover story about Lady Jonnye Mae. This moment is totally brilliant for me. I'm thinking, "Yeah, my mom's on TV again, and she's being celebrated for all to see." But immediately, that image of her begins to fade into the background, as coverage of her earlier years takes over the foreground of the tube... the poor days, the tears, the struggling days of recovering from being abandoned by her own mom while fresh with her firstborn – my sister Fe – in her belly. It was like a quintessential *Behind the Music* segment.

Then, with tears in my eyes, I turn to my sister Fe. Since my mom passed away, my sister Fe has truly taken on the soul of her. Fe's integrity and quiet strength has really allowed me to trust her and be truly bonded to her. She is now sitting next to me, and says, "I'm so glad Mom ended up on TV again before she died."

But my mom didn't die yet. She didn't just sneak off. She came back for me. "Mom came back for me, didn't she?" And my sister, with a face of absolute nurturing, says, "You can always keep learning, up to the final hour."

That statement was enormous. It was sheltering. I could not have been happier. And then I woke up. I lay there in my bed, with gentle tears streaming down my face. It was 4:20 in the morning. That middle of the night time is my major spirit connection time. It's always been that way.

I get up to go to the bathroom, thinking, "I'm so glad that dream happened the way it did. And I'm so grateful that my mom and I can still communicate and be together in some way. It's like a Night Time Dedication – her commitment to my growth." Whenever my mom shows up for me, it's almost always as if precious butterflies abound, beckoning me to be at peace.

As I float in my space of splendor sleep, the miracle of her Night Time Dedication absolutely propels me to the garden of the righteous. I once heard someone say that "if we desire to be immortal, with a truly eternal effect on the world, we will accomplish that by how rich we make our character while here on earth." I believe that the interpretation that my sister Fe gave me during the whole dream sequence speaks directly to that.

So, if what I've been told about dreams is true – that all the figures in our dreams are actual extensions of ourselves, then I am accepting that my mother showed up during my sleep to grace me with this awareness…

First, that my father, a very troubled man from a small town in the South, without the proper nurturing skills, was trying to maneuver his own power, up against a wife whose intelligence far surpassed his, by holding to the bottle and bringing not only physical abuse to his wife and children, but emotional strain and self-torture.

That this father, in his later years, became the recipient of enough grace so as to not only walk peacefully around his house, but to even finally rest there with bountiful love surrounding him. Yes, because of his willingness to change, and make things right, my father finally found that pillow of peace for his mind that had evaded him for so long.

Secondly, that my brother Tony, who had been in his own nails-to-chalkboard torture because of behavior that leaked much deception and conniving, was also able, thanks to repentance, to finally be at rest from his sorrow, amongst the utter order of that closet where he lay. Order representing the rich soil, by which all things can properly grow.

Rev. T.D Jakes asks, and I paraphrase, How is it that we can expect to allow external relationships of mess (be it with mounds of papers, or clothing, or most usually people whose contributions to our lives only breed chaos) to exist, and assume that the universe should grandly bless us with forever-hour comfort? The *mess* is only an outpicturing of what we have going on inside of us. There can surely be no internal calm until we are willing to renounce the external clutter. Then and only then will we be able to create a more harmonized outer environment.

Thirdly, my mom visions were speaking to me about the necessity of perseverance. Sometimes you get off the path, but with effort you can find your way back. And sometimes we might fall all the way down, but with focus we can rise like the phoenix. Resilience was her message. "Don't give up. Look beyond your past. Fight for your future. That's the key."

This was the word coming to me from my mother. Yes, my mother, my father, and my brother, in my dream were all *me* – the kid whom had taken a long hard journey, but who was now being prepared to finally arrive, high up for all to see, in his God predestined glory.

I used to fear death. But now I see that, continually throughout our lifetime, we *must* die to the old versions of ourselves, and that by dying to the old, we will actually ready ourselves for a more diamond-buffed deliverance, conditioned for a memorial existence. Then, possibly, we will even be able to serve someone else's future, as well as our own. I welcome it with open arms.

Some of my largest gratitude moments have come to me from the simplest things at the most unexpected times. My mom was telling me to have more faith in my current actions. My mother was a waterfall of faith. And the roots of her ways have truly guided me to fly. Like the Bluebird. The Hummingbird. And the dove.

I am so grateful, because *an angel flew in my room and*

she taught me how to fly. This is my distant Jonnye Mae today.

Mirror Bearers

"I got dressed and went to see my Dad, who had invited me over for breakfast. By the time I got there, Rosa was already gone. Watching him cook breakfast for me was really sweet. It took me back to my childhood.

When I was a kid growing up, my Dad traveled a lot for work. Usually on Saturday mornings, he'd fry up some fish he'd caught on one of his fishing trips, and he'd make grits and eggs to go with it. There we were, all those years later, and again he was cooking me breakfast. But this time felt more special than ever.

Suddenly, he stopped, got up, grabbed a

piece of paper and set it down in front of me.

'Here's the name of Gary's church. I told you I would get this for you.'

I was totally into my Dad honoring me. It felt so good to have him taking care of me in that way.

'I also told Rose you'd be calling to get Gary's phone number from her. You can go in the other room and use the phone if you want to.'

After breakfast, I went in and made the call.

I ended up speaking to my Aunt Georgene instead of my Aunt Rose. She asked me how I was doing, how I was enjoying my time with my Dad. I told her I was calling about the Gary stuff, but she knew because my Dad had already spoken to them about it.

My Aunt Georgene told me she knew what town Gary lived in, but she didn't have his phone number, and then she reiterated what my Dad had told me about Gary being a minister now.

I was reveling in the fact that I finally felt like I had some family that really had my back...

'You know, Honey,' my Aunt Georgene told me, 'at some point Punkin' might have some advice that could be useful for you...'

Punkin' is my Aunt Georgene's daughter, and she was a minister.

'You should get in touch with her,' she suggested.

This was a far cry from the Aunt Georgene who had cornered me in the bathroom when I was a kid and beaten me with a telephone cord. It felt really good to hear her looking out for me.

A couple of years before having this conversation with my Aunt Georgene about Gary, I had realized I'd really been scarred in a lot of ways by that beating I'd gotten from her when I was staying at her house. So I talked to my Dad, told him I was trying to heal all these different areas of my life, and that I needed to talk to my Aunt Georgene. I had gotten her phone number from him then. When I told her I wanted to talk to her about that beating in my childhood, she had no memory of it at all. She remembered her and Aunt Rose being perfectly lovely with me.

'You don't remember whipping me, and leaving me bleeding?'

'Ah, Honey, you know I love you…'

'It left scars on me, Georgene.'

'Now, Honey, you know we love you. We've always loved you.'

'You don't remember that you beat me

because of a phone call I'd made?'

'What phone call was that? When did you make a phone call?'

She genuinely did not remember a thing.

'You know I would never have done anything to hurt you, Baby.'

At the point in time a few years ago when I'd talked to her about the childhood beating, she was totally comforting and loving.

So when I talked to her now about Gary, we had already had our own healing and there was no reason for either of us to be guarded.

'Call Punkin', Honey. And take care of yourself.'

I was trying to digest all of these new developments and figure out what direction I needed to go.

My dad asked me, 'What are you going to do?'

'I don't know, Dad, I've got to sit with it.'

'Well, Carl, thanks for reaching out for me, and opening up to me. It means so much that you wanted to share this with me.'

This version of my Dad was so nurturing – the polar opposite of the man I'd grown up with – and it was just so lovely.

'You know I love you,' he said. 'Like I told you, I have always loved you and I always

> **will. You're my son. And like I used to say to your mama, "I love them boys more than anything." Even when you told me about your sexual things… I always loved you.'**
>
> **These warm word configurations he was putting together had nothing to do with the man I remembered from my childhood.**
>
> **I'd been out here in the world doing my whole life on my own, and so to hear my Dad sticking up for me was really huge…"**

I once heard a statement that has forever been suspended inside of me: "Relationships are the mirrors by which we see ourselves." And man, this statement is no joke. My intimate relationships have really been the ones that have kept me in the classroom teaching me about Carlton. All the games, the lessons, and the disappointments, while it would be easier to lay them against the other person, forever bring me back to *me*. I have always thought myself to be the loner, the I-prefer-my-space kind of guy. The truth is that I've been more the lost, scared type – something I've only recently been able to fully admit.

Are there justifications that could span the colors of the rainbow? Yes. You bet. For example, having to witness the struggles for love and compassion between my mother and father, as they both supported acts of delusion, deception and destruction. Like one harsh winter afternoon as my mom, my brother Tony, my cousin Phil, and I arrived home all excited with Christmas gifts, only to find my father sitting in a chair right next to the front door, in the most eerily brooding position. There he sat, with his arms tightly folded across his chest and his eyes glaring directly forward. He ordered all us kids to go into the basement. This sort of scenario was not unusual, but from his posture and the tone of his voice, I knew something more dramatic than usual was about to happen. Once we got down into the basement, we tried to distract ourselves by playing, hoping for the best.

Instantly, I hear Mom and Dad upstairs yelling at each other. The yelling turns into hard bumping and knocking sounds, and before I know it, quickly becomes a mish-mash of thumping. At the same time, my mother's voice, now screaming, swells up in my ears. We all rush back upstairs. We find my parents in a full-on fist swirling exchange. My dear mother is on the floor. She is crouched for protection, as my father – a 6'1, 195 pound man, is full-swing pounding her wherever he can, as she scrambles from corner to corner to avoid the force of his boot, kicking for any bit of flesh it can find. It was absolutely horrifying.

That time was different. It was the first time I was actually witnessing the fighting I had only heard – and heard about – before.

My parents had the quintessential love/hate dynamic. Yes, they stayed living in the same house, making one statement – that we truly care for each other, and want to be together – but then their fighting revealed a much different yearning from their souls. And I was never really clear on who to blame for these brawling sessions.

On the one hand, my mother was having me keep the

secret of her private bank account, and having me ride around in the back seat of Leon's car. He was her lover – a forever-dear-to-her ex-convict who'd been in and out of prison for murder. I loved Leon because he always treated my mom like a diamond, but I remember sitting in the back of his car with my fists clenched down into the seat, and my shoulders raised high, nervous that my dad might drive by and see us all together. I loved my dad, but I loved Leon more because he never hurt my mom.

At the same time, my mom shared with me how she had found a multitude of other ladies' phone numbers in my father's clothing pockets. She also found receipts in the glove compartment of my father's car, revealing purchases for appliances and furniture that never saw the light of *our* house because, as I was to find out not too much later when my mom confronted him and he confessed, my dad was secretly supporting a second family.

My father told me that he was doing what he was doing, and was forced into beating on my mother, because she was the cheater. What was I to believe? Should love exist with no pain? Should a true love relationship be free of deception? Should the voice of someone saying "I want you as my partner" be enough for one to trust? I had no way of answering those questions. My private schooling gave me nothing to be proud of. The whole thing was flat out wrong. And while I don't want to have to lay fault at the feet of my parents, and while I'm the first one to say that boxes are not spaces to place anyone in, sometimes you've got to call the thing for what it is. Sometimes some things just are, and need to be acknowledged as *black and white.*

Did the turbulent situation with my parents during my formative years skew my understanding about the whole heart union thing? Yes. And were there any healthy role models guiding me as a young man, as I sought the comfort of other men? No, there weren't. But all that seems foolish to keep spouting out, because now I am a fully grown man, and I have been one for quite some time, with access to all kinds of resources and healthy relationships – be they straight or gay – which can serve as awesome, soul-bonding guideposts.

"Love is a beautiful thing" is a fantastic statement, but love is only a beautiful thing if you know how to receive it and give it properly. And clearly I did not. So I simply hung myself on the tree of "I don't need it…" I was playing cameo Carlton roles in all my relationships. And the stuff got deep. I think back on those times in my Silverlake apartment with that Salvation Army floral-print sofa, and that egg-shaped yard sale coffee table; with the remnants of marijuana and even harder drugs strewn about. They remain so Twilight-Zone-zoom-lensed in my think box… Ashy ankles dangling around the edges of the furniture, ass and balls so free and hungry they were screaming to be acknowledged, and sweat rollin' over dark skin, shaved skin, pale skin, even skin that housed anger and abuse – they all became my resting place.

Of course, I see things differently now – or I should say, more truthfully – and thank God for that. The old ways never did really offer me peace. I tell you, my mind-mirror has been cleaned, and covered over, and cleaned, again and again; as I have extended myself from one person to another, be it for a full-moon one-time thing, or for something of a more lasting duration. And while I have sometimes wished my tarnished mirror would be taken away to some far and distant antique store, I am actually very grateful she's still around – allowing me now to know myself just a little bit better.

Like I said, this statement is no joke: "Relationships are the mirrors by which we see ourselves." How I love, how far I can love, and how much I have known nothing about love, have all been revealed to me through that deep and penetrating mind reflector.

The Full Throttle Course

"When I returned from my trip to Augusta and found myself back in Los Angeles - and back in reality - it really hit me.

'Holy shit! Now that I've opened this can of worms and gotten all of Gary's contact information, now what?'

Throughout the years, I had entertained thoughts that it might serve me to confront Gary, but I could never figure out how to make that happen. Now I didn't really have that excuse anymore. Considering the way everything had unfolded in Augusta, what was I going to do about it?

In ballet class one day, I was sharing about my trip with a lady I had started to date a little bit before I went to visit my Dad. She was a dancer. She was very talented, and she really stood out in class, and so naturally she was the kind of person I would be drawn to. We sort of had a little energy between us, and what was happening with her was happening during a year I had set aside to be celibate – a time that was all about me getting clear on my sexuality.

With getting clear on my sexuality as my goal, I was interested in platonically dating – and that meant either sex. And here was this sexy female, and I didn't know what it could be. I thought, 'Let's see what being with a woman does for me at this stage of my life. Does it ignite me? Repel me?' So we had a couple of dates, went to the movies. I was really into it. I always enjoy being the man to a woman in the times I have been with ladies.

At the same time, I was aware that I was in a quandary with myself, and I was apprehensive to let her know how much I was on the fence sexually.

After I got back from my trip, we talked about what had come up for me in Georgia. She told me she had gone through something similar to what I'd been through with Gary, and she had ended up getting involved with attorneys that helped her deal with her thing.

'Attorneys? Are you serious?'

'Yeah,' she told me, 'and if you need some information, I have someone here in Los Angeles I can connect you to.' She was very supportive.

So I got the lawyer's phone number from her and called the guy.

The first thing the attorney did was to check the registries to see if Gary was registered anywhere as a sex offender.

'I can't find him listed anywhere,' the lawyer told me.

'Really?' That seemed to me like a big red flag.

Then the attorney asked me some very specific questions, and found out the entire period of molestation had happened in Florida.

'In that case, Carlton, this will have to be handled by the Florida court system. I will get you the number for the Special Investigations Division there.'

He gets me the number. I get on the phone with them. I tell them my initial plan. 'Listen, I'm a professional actor. And I was thinking…'

I tell them the whole scenario I have in my

mind. I would go back to Florida, show up at Gary's church, and do a badass acting job. I would get myself to one of his church services, find the perfect moment, and break down into some fantastic crying episode that would naturally require me to have to talk to the pastor.

'So then, once I have a private audience with Gary, and we are the only two people in the room,' I explain to the investigator, 'I dry my tears, snap off my actor face, and say, "Do you remember who I am?"'

As for me and my lady friend, since I'd been gone on my trip, there was that built-in distance between us, and I kept that distance in place. It's not like I came to some concrete decision one way or another about my sexual orientation. I didn't make a decision to not be with her, exactly. I just naturally seemed to need so much space for myself upon my return from Georgia, it just bled into me creating even more distance between us.

I never did reveal to her that I had been with guys.

It was kind of ironic. There I was, fantasizing about asking Gary, 'Do you remember who I am?' At the same time, I was trying to answer that question for myself. Who was I, really?"

"Vogue. Let your body move to the music. Hey, hey. hey. Come on, vogue. Let your body go with the flow. You know you can do it..."

Those were the words streaming from the lips of The "Blond Ambition" gal herself – as the so-named world tour launched us into a live performance version of her hit song, for viewers exceeding some 80,000 plus. And those were the words that were being chanted, so that I might also claim more freedom for myself.

Long before I ever found myself on the "Blond Ambition" tour, I found myself dreaming Madonna dreams, somewhere in the mid-1980s in Printers Row on Dearborn Street in downtown Chicago. That is where I got initially cast into deliberate focus toward this music legend.

There I was, standing outside Orly's restaurant, where I was working at the time as a waiter. And it was while resting outside, taking a cigarette break, that I saw Madonna's face boldly covering a full page spread for that week's Sunday paper release. The article was featuring her then-tour, *Who's That Girl*, which had swept its way into Chicago.

I remember reading the article, thinking instantly about how a guy from Chicago had gone on to become Michael Jackson's lead dancer, *and how I wished I could be that for a music celebrity one day.* I had the image of Madonna in my hands, as I was thinking those sweet thoughts – never realizing that later, many years later, *I would actually be the selected dancer literally holding Madonna,* over and over again, not only in my hands, but far over my head.

For me, some of the greatest moments with her happened as we were in the stadiums at around 4:00 in the afternoon, watching the early-arrival fans rush as fast as they could to the front of the stage. We'd always have the piped-in soulful sounds of Lisa Stansfield blaring through the speakers as we prepared to move from one song to the next, making sure all was in order for our soon-to-come late night explosion. Those proved to be true hallelujah revelation times for me.

Madonna's calm before the storm of celebration moved me much. As did knowing that we'd all come a long way, through the rehearsal/training days. This full throttle, excellence-to-the-effort process that M promoted, was a lesson that I knew I had to maintain for the rest of my life. *For every aspect of my living.* We were resting in shimmer-possessed confidence. No discount, dime store dedications from us – we were delivering hard core, rock-em-sock-em quality.

"Gene Kelly. Fred Astaire. Ginger Rogers. Dance on air..." Madonna continues singing.

We surely can't arrive on top of any cloud if our focus is not on that *excellence* course of action. And there surely would never have been a Jamie Foxx, Halle Berry, Mary J. Blige, Oprah Winfrey, Denzel Washington, Sidney Poitier, Magic Johnson, Condoleezza Rice, Barack Obama, or Martin Luther King Jr., to lead the atoms of our mind into jubilation had they not all been championing this very noteworthy cause – *the pursuit of excellence.*

But I've also grown to realize that *many times, while*

striving for excellence, we will encounter much persecution. In the beginning, it was Madonna's life that was, for me, a prime example of this fact… the way she stood the test of time – against slander, and lawsuits, and downright ugly criticism… but now I realize I've come full circle, *and it is in my own life, on so many stages, that I now find this very same truth, played out,* front and center.

I understand now that all of the ridicule, intensity, confusion, and grandeur that surrounded my life were established to support me being ripened for a very large purpose. I understand now about strength of character, and how that speaks volumes. This was learning I had to acquire from experiential circumstances. And not from some lofty intellectual conceptualizing.

True leadership, as John C. Maxwell, in his book "Leadership 101" states, is largely contingent upon one's ability to be trustworthy. For me, his book punctuated the importance of making the distinction between whether someone is to be *trusted,* or merely *tolerated.* This has often times been a difficult beast for me to wrestle down. Trustworthiness dictates the level of intimacy possible with another person. I can tolerate almost anyone but that doesn't mean I'm going to let them in.

Since I was a kid, it has always been my desire to be a man who would have enough power to serve our society with more and more life-evolving knowledge. And I am absolutely clear now that there's no way I could ever expect someone to fully tune into my thoughts if they did not truly trust that what I was speaking about was something I had authentically lived through. People can smell our truth no matter how much we try to cover it with a floralized façade.

In addition to the issue of trustworthiness, Maxwell also professes that our ability to maintain a commitment to a leader, and the lasting effects the leader can have, are also impacted by their ability to show genuine interest in the people they are linked to. And as the buffet of slow-drip remembrances resurfaces in me, I reflect on my years with the Golden Beauty, how she offered many surprising moments of caring and sharing, and expressions of generosity – and how I am now finding and growing those same seeds in my own character.

Because of Madonna's acts of kindness, because of all of her domino-ing deliverings and sharings designed to mentor me – gifts that felt like Vegas casino jackpot wins – I absolutely reached a level of dedication to her that surprised even me. And even the harder-to-swallow lessons I learned in my years spent around her created no diminishment of my dedication to her.

And now, as I find inside myself that same kind of Empowerer with the potential for creating lasting impact in the world, *I am reaching that same level of dedication to my own character and my own blasted-wide-open path.*

Meeting my Empowerer on all the stages of my own life, finding him inside me at every turn, I know I am in the flow… "Let your body move to the music. Hey, hey, hey. Come on, vogue, let your body go with the flow. You know you can do it…"

Released, delivered, healed, strengthened, empowered, and lifted up by Spirit, *I know I will do it,* as Spirit moves me from old shadows into the light at the heart of my own life. For it is there, from that place of Truth, that I can live, *truly front and center.*

The Walk of Responsibility

You know it when you see it
It's like that perfect pony on display
Like that glide of the gallant matador
Or that gait of
the Knight to the Dame

Each one is poised with carefulness
allowing nothing to make it sway from
its mission that will be glorified
by the choices made along the way

The walk of responsibility is
one of truth and pride
founded by moves
of high purpose
It offers few traces of spaces for compromise

The walk of responsibility
can move us to the other side
But we must release our ways that trample
then say YES to the accountability stride

The Voice of Frederick

"'So, that's what I'm going to do. I'll show up at his church…'

The detective told me essentially, no problem, just figure out when you're going to come down.

'When you get here, we'll probably wire you, where you're wearing a microphone under your pants.' It seemed like some wild movie segment.

That was it. It was all planned out. And I sure was all excited about it. It was going to be a full-on detective drama. Knowing the trip was coming up, I made myself get up every day for two and a half months and go into nature on prayer walks. I knew I needed to really be prayed up in order to deal with what was coming. From the end of November, 2005, until February, 2006 when I went to Florida, I stayed very prayerful.

I felt like I returned from visiting my Dad with Pandora's Box wide open. I knew I needed to be serious about putting the whole situation under God's guidance. And while I was definitely trying to be forgiving about all this stuff, I really had no idea how I was going to feel when I was actually sitting or standing in front of Gary. I had so many areas of my damaged life connected to him.

I didn't know how my anger would show up or how thick it would be when it did. It occurred to me that I had never really faced the depths of my frustration and anger toward Gary. I had been dealing with the way it made me feel about myself – my own shame – but never my anger toward Gary.

Before I started talking to the detective, I never really realized how pissed off I had been. I had never before let that emotion be real.

The detectives were asking me, 'Who are you? Why do you really want to come down here and face Gary?' They were investigating my credibility, and I could see their point. For all they knew, I could be planning to show up at Gary's church with a gun in my pocket, pull out the gun, and blow fifteen people away – just like that.

It was strange but it wasn't until they started asking me those kinds of questions, and investigating who I was in this situation, that I realized, 'Okay, good, good. I'm not that crazy. I may be finally feeling my anger towards Gary, but at least I'm not that angry – not dangerously angry.'

So then we set the date for the trip.

I arrived in Florida on February 8, 2006.

I checked into the local Motel 6. We had planned that I was to meet with the detectives that same afternoon. When I arrived in the morning, I was on pins and needles. I left them messages, letting them know I had arrived. I restlessly awaited their return call to me. I was pacing around my room, trying to watch TV, trying to stretch, basically doing whatever to try and relax myself. When nobody called me back, I started freaking out.

My mind was whirling. 'Hadn't they told me we would definitely have a meeting that afternoon? Had they set me up? What if I had spent the money on the plane ticket, checked into the hotel for the week, and then ended up waiting around, day after day, for their phone call?' I really started spinning. 'Was I going to have to go through with my plan on my own?'

I had scheduled this Florida trip around some work in Orlando that was supposed to start that Friday – three days away. So there I was, not in the greatest part of town, with three extra days before my gig, and all I could think was, 'Please, don't blow me off.'

At 5:30, my phone rang. It was a different detective than the one I had been dealing with up to that point. When I was in Los Angeles, I had been speaking to a detective who was the head of the Special Investigations Division. By the time I got to Florida, they had apparently appointed a specific detective to my case, and this was who was on the phone now.

He asked me, 'Can you get together around 8:30?'

'You mean 8:30 tonight?' That seemed a bit strange to me – meeting at night. 'I guess so. Sure.'

'Since it's going to be after hours,' he continued, 'you will have to ring a special buzzer so that someone can let you in.'

8:30 comes. I am standing outside in the dark. I ring the buzzer.

A voice tells me, 'Someone will be down

to get you.'

I'm waiting around, loitering in the dark. Ten minutes pass, twenty minutes, twenty-five minutes.

Fully armed sheriffs are leaving, and they are looking at me. I'm thinking, 'This is all really crazy. Here I am, the black guy hanging around in the dark.'

Any time I am aware that I am the black dude standing around in the dark late at night, I wonder, 'What are they thinking when they look at me? What kind of shit is going through their minds? Is this scramble of me having to first wait hours for their return call, and now having to wait for someone to come downstairs – is this all a sign that this whole thing isn't going to go well?'

When the guy finally comes down and acknowledges me, he is very nice.

My mind snaps into place. I say to myself, 'Alright, Dude, you are fucking all the way in this now. There is absolutely no turning back. If you change your mind now, they are going to be on you. They know what you look like.'

I realized I had crossed a line. I couldn't dodge anything now – even if I wanted to.

I'm walking in after hours. It's a huge room with a lot of different desks. It is totally surreal. There are two or three other people at their desks. I go deeper into racial consciousness. The detective is a big white guy, and I am a big black dude, and he is walking me into the room.

First into one room. Then into another room. There is an advocate, another white guy, in the room who is there on behalf of the abused person – and in that case, it was me. The advocate is there as a witness.

Heads look up at me.

I ask myself, 'Are they thinking I am the bad guy? Here are these guys with fucking guns on their hips. And what are they thinking about me? Do they see me as the bad black guy?'

In Los Angeles, or on the streets of Chicago, I always have the same thought. It's like the movie, *Crash*. When two black guys are on the street, who, exactly, needs to be afraid? These white folks see black folks and think they need to be afraid, but who is the minority to the larger percentage? As a black man, I've always been aware of the fact that it's fifty thousand whites to two of us blacks.

Honestly, who is the one who needs to be afraid?"

"If I could..." Now, tell me there's not a thousand ways to fill in that blank. For me, my "If I could..." speaks right to the realm of strength. I'm talking about a Lauryn Hill for MTV's "Unplugged" meets Brad Pitt in *Fight Club* kind of strength.

Maybe for you, the missing piece is an "If I could…" related to knowing how to make the most amazing triple layer German chocolate cake. Or, maybe it's an "If I could…" related to going on the most luxurious vacation, where cascades of water wait patiently to engulf you in their warm blanket of loveliness. Or, maybe it's as simple as desiring to have someone hold you in an ever so tender way.

For me, it's about the way Lauryn unfolds herself, with anger and frustration piercing so honestly through every cell of her being, or the way Brad goes right for the jugular, ripe to sustain any degree of force thrown back at him while simultaneously holding a smile – these things just truly warm my heart. The way I experience each of them, I get the feeling that in order to do their masterful work, they have dialed down their normal selves and called up an alter ego – in keeping with the goals and mission of the fight club depicted in the film.

Many times in my life I have had to also use a similar tool, and construct an alter ego. For me, my other self is a bad-ass named Frederick. The name may sound a bit proper, but make no mistake – my Frederick takes political correctness and throws it far out the window. Much like Brad in *Fight Club* and Lauryn for "Unplugged," Frederick often speaks with a harsh tone and without a single note of intended apology.

Today he rises up and reaches right for the area of my life occupied by my siblings. His position holds steady with my sister, Valencia, nicknamed Candi by my mother because, apparently, my mother's first thoughts when Valencia came out were that she seemed as sweet as candy. As I've gotten older, I've realized that often, my Candi is the bittersweet type of morsel.

Frederick chimes in, saying "When you were back in Chicago, why did you let Candi's obviously boxed-up views about your sexuality clam you up? As if she's the chosen authority. Think about this," he continues, "She's supposed to be the one all deep into the Jesus thing – which is supposed to be about unconditional love and compassion, right? Well, then, why was she consciously choosing to stay pissed at your brother, Tony, for all those years? Just because emotionally he couldn't pull it together fast enough after your mother died?"

He goes on. "Sure, maybe Tony hoarded some things he'd found in your mom's apartment – a precious ring, some other things. Whatever. And no, of course he should not have manipulated a takeover of the family house only to discover that he couldn't maintain it financially. True, your family lost ownership of the house where you grew up. But, hell, the man lost his mind for a spell! I mean your mother fuckin' died! Clearly, Tony wasn't thinking straight. Don't you think Candi, if she is at all true to her Godliness, should have been more forgiving? Or at least sympathetic to him?"

You see, that's the tricky thing about my sister Valencia.

Or Candi – depending upon how she's making me feel. In many ways she can be the most caring, loving person. Like beginning in the late 1990s right through about 2004, when I was having such a hard time. She was incredibly supportive, came through with money to help me along, freely offered moments of prayer, and words of wisdom. Then I look at the callousness she projected towards my brother, and it's hard to reconcile. It just doesn't seem to fit. That's when Frederick starts in on me again.

"And," he reminds me, "don't forget Puerto Rico. There you were having the most incredible time of your career, sharing your blessings, and Miss Sweet Candi spits out that ridiculous attitude towards that woman who so generously offered to be your personal chef three to four days a week at no cost. Why the fuck did she do that? What was that about?"

I remember that moment vividly. I was so caught off guard. "I don't know, Carlton," Frederick pipes up, "you'd better give it some thought. Do you think you can trust her?"

There I was, sharing with her what was clearly a profound time for me, and what does she do? She goes right into suspicion and negativity. She sailed right past any kind of acknowledgment that in the offering of free services from the cook, God may have been brilliantly gracing me. Laying on my pillow-layered King sized bed, smelling the ocean, trying to be at one with the soothing salt water erupting from the beautiful crystalline Atlantic waves on the opposite side of my wide open balcony door, I was all sadness and disappointment. I almost felt like crying.

It was so strange. On the one hand, I knew what I knew about how God was showing up for me and all. On the other hand, what should I make of what Frederick was telling me about Mrs. Church Lady? Why was she coming from such a dark place, my bittersweet Candi?

I thought back to a day when I was driving down Pacific Coast Highway with Candi, who had come out to Los Angeles to visit me. There we were, brother and sister, ready for a peaceful, heart-bonding afternoon at the beach, the electric sun just oozing suggestions of nurturing. I had taken her that morning to my church, wanting to share with her a place that meant so much to me.

Here is what transpired between us after attending Agape, my church, named for unconditional love. "I just think people should dress up when they go to church," she said. "It's not right to show up for God that way." Unbelievable. She ended up getting all caught up in what people were wearing, as if everyone at Agape was wearing piss-stained potato sacks for clothes. Such a beautiful day ahead of us and she had to lead us into some ridiculous conversation about proper clothing etiquette for fellowshipping with God.

Frederick darts in with, "Yeah, man, come the fuck on! What you need to just accept is that, yeah, maybe people might say they're all about the God thing. They might even have many more years in it than you do, but it does not mean they truly have it together. Just look at your sister. God is about Love, Love, and only Love, no matter who you are, what you wear, or what sex you're pumpin'. Remember, in James 2:1-9, the Bible [NIV Version] says straight out that favoritism is forbidden:

> 'My brothers, as believers in our glorious Lord Jesus Christ, don't show favoritism. Suppose a man comes into your meeting wearing a gold ring and fine clothes, and a poor man in shabby clothes also comes in. If you show special attention to the man wearing fine clothes and say, "Here's a good seat for you," but say to the poor man, "You stand here," or "Sit on the floor by my feet," have you not discriminated among yourselves and become judges with evil thoughts? Listen, my dear brothers: Has not God chosen those who are poor in the eyes of the world to be rich in faith and to inherit the kingdom he promised those who love him? But you have insulted the poor. Is it not the rich who are exploiting you? Are they not the ones who are dragging you into court? Are they not the ones who are slandering the noble name of him to whom you belong? If you really keep the royal law found in scripture, "Love your neighbor as yourself," you are doing right. But if you show favoritism, you sin and are convicted by the law as lawbreakers.'

Then Frederick blurts out, "Especially in regards to

who you sleep with, man. Honestly, not one of the Ten Commandments says anything about sexual orientation. Nothing at all. And aren't the Ten Commandments supposed to be the most important character standards in the Bible? And besides," he goes on to say, "I don't think it is anybody's job to go around judging others, especially when what someone is doing is not in any way taking away from anyone else's well being or livelihood. God wants us to be here, to lay down Love to one another, and leave the judging to Him. All of that other stuff is just a crock of shit."

I told you alter egos can be a bit harsh. Still, what Frederick was saying seemed like the truth to me. Either you have faith that God is a loving and forgiving God or you don't. Where does it say that we are supposed to place our faith in what does or does not appear to be perfect around us? Isn't our faith supposed to be in the covenant of the Word? I believe it's got to be.

Over the years, as I watched myself sit in frustration with my sister's ways, I must admit that I began to realize I was letting myself become guilty of the very things I found fault with in her. I had to learn to accept that the trials I was going through with her were calling me to strengthen my own loving and compassionate ways. Our relationship was laying the groundwork for me to learn not be rocked by outside opinions of whatever might be going on with me.

My life is, was, and always needs to be, about my own intimate relationship with God. I am to answer to Him and to no one else. And if He wants me doing things in a different way, I am sure He will make that known to me and flip me around.

Yes, many times, Frederick, my powerful alter ego, has stepped in, snapped me out of old ways of thinking and snapped me right into a more proactive approach. In these conversations I had with him about my sister, he was speaking strongly to me about honoring my emotions. And as usual, I actually needed him to blast me a bit.

The conclusion I've come to is that, "If I could," I would live my life as Frederick, twenty-four/seven. This is my wish, and more than my wish, *it is my truth.* And my ultimate goal.

Oh, Irony

"Walking into the detective's offices, feeling all that race consciousness going through my mind, something came up for me from the last year I was with Gary.

The Gary thing only happened in the summers, and it was during that last summer that I had started teaching dance. My oldest brother, Bobie, and I were teaching at Dingbats Disco in Chicago. It was my first ever dance job.

Every Saturday, we taught kiddy disco lessons to Jewish kids preparing to be bar mitzvahed. I was thirteen years old, too, but I definitely wasn't going to be having a bar mitzvah to mark my passage into manhood. We had our own ways of proving our manhood on the streets of Chicago.

Anyway, there I was with my brother, on Saturdays during the disco era. Bobie, who was nineteen years old at the time, and I, would show up and perform a disco dance number. We would choreograph the whole thing. After we did our number, we would teach some dances to the kids. As I spent time around the Jewish kids who were there to learn disco from me, I remember thinking, 'Would what happened to me with Gary have happened if I'd been a Jewish kid from a family with money?'

Little did I know as we were teaching pieces of The Hustle and The Bus Stop to these kids that on my Mom's side of the family, I had actually come from a long line of black Jews. Then, many years later, while taking Kabbalah classes, I got invited to Shabbat sundown services on Friday and Saturday nights.

Around that same time, my Jewish girlfriend, Andrea, who I actually introduced to Kabbalah, called me to say she had something major to share with me. She then showed up at my place and produced a large envelope of downloaded images revealing what she had

discovered – pictures of a black synagogue in Chicago which was supposedly the third largest synagogue in the whole nation. It was wild to see all these black folks wearing yarmulkes on their heads.

My Mom was from Chicago. Was my Jewish ancestry linked to this synagogue? I kept thinking how wild that would be.

But for the moment, I am still thirteen years old, and all I know is that here are all these kids from this entirely different lifestyle being brought in to my class. There I am, being repeatedly molested by Gary, teaching disco dance lessons to these kids as they're getting anointed to go to the next level in their life, and I can't help but wonder, 'Does anything like this ever happen to them?'"

Kabbalah. What a powerful tool for living. This ancient teaching, some two thousand years old, originated from writings established in the Torah, and guides one past sitting in a position of whining and moaning about what's not right in one's day to day affairs. It teaches us to focus not on what's been done to us in the past, but to accept that we, through our own thinking, sculpt the mold for our lives. I, myself, spent a year and a half trying to grip my mind around some of the Kabbalah concepts, and I'm grateful to say that many things about my actions did shine through for me with incredible clarity.

When I first discovered Kabbalah, I never thought about the irony that would later come to me, wholly linking the teachings themselves with Madonna – the very channel chosen to deliver me to Kabbalah in the first place. Madonna introduces me to Kabbalah, and then the Universe presents me with a situation in which the biggest Kabbalah lesson of my life plays itself out in a scenario between the two of us.

My relationship with Madonna began in 1990 when I was selected to accompany her as a dancer on the *Blond Ambition* tour. Close to five hundred male dancers were called to audition, all hoping to land one of the coveted positions as "the chosen few" – eight to be exact – for a worldwide traveling experience.

At the audition, we were taught three different dance combinations, all intended to show off specific, necessary movement elements, which Madonna was planning to showcase in her larger-than-life stage show. I showed up with absolute relaxation. This job was mine. *There was nothing that was going to get in my way.* I was quite confident. I was already in negotiations for a tour with Whitney Houston, and that was the added security I needed to feel confident that I could grab a prized position on The Material Girl's tour.

I arrived at the audition dressed in a pair of shredded denim jeans, a cut-off-at-the-sleeves flannel shirt, a leather biker jacket, and a pair of sneaker-like dance shoes. That was the look back then. To my surprise, Madonna was actually in the room, along with her choreographer, Vince

Patterson. She was sporting a somewhat sloppy pony tail, a pair of denim cut-off hot pants, a wife beater t-shirt, fishnet stockings, and combat boots. Damn, she sure did look good.

Over and over again, we went through the routines – some stylized stuff, and some very technical dance moves. *We wore that room out.* There was sweat flowin' from every part of our bodies. She sat in a chair the whole time, directing steps the way she thought they ought to be done. We were dramatically throwing ourselves on the floor, then back up again, into outrageous moves – double outside turns, a foot curling around the back of the knee, arms swirling over the head – that kind of thing. Then we'd go into fully flowing moves that carried us quickly across the floor, then into some high-brow posing positions that fit perfectly with the throbbing remix of her then-hit, "Vogue." The audition went on like this for nearly four and a half hours, and throughout the process, they would make the necessary cuts, eliminating dancers.

The day continued on, we danced some more, they made more cuts, we danced harder, and they cut even deeper. This went on until about twelve guys were left standing. The heat was on. And by the time we got to that stage of the process, the other guys were layin' out some of their best work – as determined as I was to win over the pop diva. When the day was finally over, life for me never seemed better. That was it? I couldn't believe that just one day of dance was all that was going to be required of me in order for them to make their picks. Or, so I thought.

Later that evening, after I'd come in from dinner, I found a message on my answering machine from the Blond Vixen herself, saying "Hey, I'm trying to reach Carlton. It's Madonna. Listen, I'm going out to a club tonight, and was wondering if you could meet me there. Let me know, okay? Call me and I'll give you the info. My number is... Call me, okay? *You better call me!*" That sort of sour playfulness was just her way. I never did figure out how she got my personal phone number, but I was just happy she did. I was so excited, I was bouncing all around my apartment, like some lonely puppy freshly released from a kennel. It was a Friday night, the call had come from Madonna The Music Icon herself, and so of course I was going to show up.

We met at a hotspot called Club Louie, a raw urban underground kind of scene, a narrow 1970s tavern-type space, very dark, with the smells of sweat and incense throughout. We had a blast, drinking, laughing and dancing our butts off. There were a few other guys who joined us as well, a few of whom I recognized from the audition. We partied it up that night.

Margaritas and Long Island iced teas were flowin' hard. Madonna was having a good time getting lost in the music, from partner to partner. And the crowd in the club was loving the fact that she was even there at all. And for me, it was just blowing my mind. As the night neared the end, Madonna mentioned to me that there was a dance class she was going to take on Sunday and she wanted to know if I could make it there. She presented it as a question, but I was no fool. I knew what she meant.

Sunday arrived, and there I was stepping in to take this class, which I knew nothing about, from some teacher I had never heard of. I arrived at the studio fifteen minutes early to warm up and get my mind prepared, something I normally did whenever I'd go take a class. With Madonna involved, I really didn't know what was going to go down. And I surely was not about to take any chances. For the first few minutes, I found myself in the studio by myself – no teacher, no other students, just me.

The class was supposed to start at 10:00 a.m., but come 10:00, I was still alone, starting to think, "What's going on? Did I get the time wrong? Was it supposed to be yesterday? Why was the door already open? Was this some sort of twisted joke set-up? My brain was beginning to spin, creating a whirling nervousness throughout my body.

Then, at about 10:15, I hear the front door open, and in walks this guy, smiling and apologizing for being late. He introduces himself as the teacher, and then like a perfectly rehearsed scene, in walks Madonna, dressed in oversized, cut-off at the knee, "cholo" shorts, signature wife beater t-shirt, sweatshirt tied at her hips, and a pair of Nike running shoes. Everything turned out as planned, and I was thrilled.

The teacher stalled, waiting for the other students to show up, and started the class after about another fifteen minutes. Seven more students did eventually trail in, and the class commenced. It was actually more of a hip-hop class, and though it wasn't the most natural style for me, I bucked up and held my own. And what a blast it was, to be in an actual dance class, watching Madonna learn everything right along with the rest of us. All of this seemed too good to be real. The class lasted about an hour, and everybody seemed pleased as we all tried to cool down from the high energy and heat that broke out in the room.

I stayed on the dance floor, standing up close to the mirror, changing my wet t-shirt. I thought it would be a perfect set-up for Madonna to get an eye full of me all wet and bare-chested. Right on cue, she came right up to me, staring me down. She hesitated for a minute, and then said, "So, are you interested in goin' on tour with me?" She gave me no breath of space to respond. "If you are, then you have to cut that hair."

Again, she had that somewhat serious playfulness thing about her. She was referring to my fairly sloppy dreadlocks. But I didn't care. I knew this was my moment! She was saying "Yes" to me for the job, and without wasting a beat, I said, "Yeah, I'm totally into it. And changing my hair is no big deal. It's just hair!" She held a beat, and then with a kind of curious smile, she said "Okay, then… I guess I'll be talking to you later." And with a turn that mimicked her on-stage persona, she made her way out of the studio.

All of this was so much the kind of thing I had dreamt about for years, but I could never have even imagined it would feel so good. That, for sure, was a blast-off day for me. It was the beginning of a working/friendship relationship that would span a solid ten years.

Back to the irony I mentioned at the beginning of this chapter, as to how the path that got me to Kabbalah was linked to the very teachings of Kabbalah.

I traveled the world with Madonna for two separate tours – the *Blond Ambition* tour, which included many award show appearances, filming the music video "Vogue," and a commercial for Nike which never did actually air because of red state religious issues; and *The Girlie Show* tour. Ten years whizzed by, slamming me right up against the year 2000 – time for her to embark on her next world excursion – *The Drowned Tour*.

I was not really sure if it was right for me to even contemplate going out on tour with her again, because of an earlier incident with her that left me feeling quite uneasy, related to a decision I had made to present to Madonna's production company a script I had developed which I thought could be a very cool vehicle for Madonna and me to do together.

The way the whole script thing had been handled just made no sense to me at all. I had never before felt disrespected by Madonna or her people – but I sure did in this situation. My fear was running wild and my frustration was beginning to rage. Why did it have to be this way? Why, why, why? I guess some things we're just never meant to know.

Flash forward to Madonna's *Drowned Tour*. I began to hear rumors that she was going back out on tour and I had heard through the grapevine that they might be calling me. I'm thinking, Yeah, sure, that will be the day. What am I going to say if they do call? Will I be able to stand my ground and admit, in front of Madonna, the woman who had helped me pay my bills, how pissed off I'd been? I was starting to feel just way too vulnerable inside, especially since I was low on money and needed another job badly. Then again, how could I even consider not saying something, after what had gone down? All of this was cycling through my brain at rapid speed.

I remember talking to Joseph, a good buddy of mine, and saying to him, "I'm just going to stop trippin' about it, and I'm saying to God right now, 'If it's meant for me to forgive them and stay in this relationship for another tour, then I will. But if it is time for me to move on and start my own career *really*, then that's what I'll do, God. Just make it absolutely clear to me.'"

That's what I said. Well, you know that old saying, "Be careful what you ask for," and I wished I had remembered it and given it more serious thought because I was about to learn its truth, and learn it fast.

Days rolled by, and then one lovely Saturday morning, with birds chirping blissfully to the air, that long-awaited call finally made its way to me. I heard the voice on the other end and recognized it right away. It was Madonna's manager. She began rambling on, and I just held the phone and listened to see where she was going with all of it. Eventually, she led into asking me if I might be into "going out again" on tour. I was a bit flabbergasted. I stalled for a couple of seconds, all stuttered up inside, while pretending to be okay about hearing from her. Never once did I decide to confront her about what had happened regarding my movie script. Regardless of my inner turmoil, a somewhat regrettable "Yes" leaked out of me, and I found myself saying "Sure, I'll show up to the callback audition and meet the new director."

A whole week passed before I was to meet with them. Madonna was there again, acting as if nothing ever happened. I did my dance thing, and everything seemed status quo. They kept me until the end, pairing me up with almost every other dancer there. "Carlton, stand next to this person. Carlton, do the combination with them again." Their configurations just continued on and on.

Once they were done with their pairings, the director's assistant turned to me and, stopping the entire room, asked out loud, "Carlton, can you *really* do this?" The intent of the question was to determine whether I could clear a three month opening in my schedule in just the two days before we were due to start rehearsals. I responded with a reassuring, "Yes." She replied, "Are you sure? We start on Monday." I was caught off guard but again, I responded, "Yes. Absolutely." She said, "Okay, are you *sure* you can do this?" This time I was really wondering what all the back and forth repetitive questioning was about, but again I chimed in with my defiant "Yes."

Anyway, from the table, they continued on discussing whatever details they had to for a bit longer, and then that was it. They thanked everyone for coming, and the day was over. As I grabbed my bag to leave, the director approached me to say, "It was so great to see you. How have you been? Nice to have you here... blah, blah, blah... I'll be seeing you soon."

Now, considering that stream of events, anyone in their

right mind would be thinking the job was a go, and that's where my head was, without a doubt. But, to my dismay, from the audition on Friday through the weekend, I never did get a call as to whether or not I would be starting rehearsals on Monday. In fact, there never was, ever, any phone call saying "Yes, you're going," or "No, you're not, I'm sorry." Nothing. The whole equation just made no sense to me whatsoever.

Who's to say why it was all handled the way it was? I do know that for me, if it was just about her wanting to go in a different creative direction, I'm not naïve. I get that. Or, whatever the reasons could have been – fine. I say, "Just please tell me something." I was feeling nothing but *red fury.*

I had always been respectful to Madonna. I was on time for every rehearsal. I never slacked off during a performance. Even in my private times, I would never get into gossiping with other people about her. And even while she was going through her legal dispute with some of the other dancers about *Truth or Dare,* I stood my ground to honor her so that she would not be taken advantage of.

Then my brain rewound to that phone conversation I'd had with my buddy Joseph. I was remembering that *I had put out a request to God to make it absolutely clear which direction I should go.* And then all the pieces came together. I then saw through all the behavior of the Madonna camp and realized that God had indeed gifted me with exactly the answer I needed. I asked for it to be made clear and *that it was.* No question about it. This was a true Kabbalah process knocking hard at my door, screaming at me, "Take responsibility for your choices."

"How had my own choices figured into the equation of all the insanity?" There I'd been, so furious about the way my script had been handled, and the confusion surrounding the audition. But hadn't I asked for a sign? A very clear sign as to which direction I was meant to go? And isn't that exactly what I got from the way I was handled – an absolutely clear, impossible to ignore, *sign*? So, then, why was I pouting and moaning? Through this whole scenario I truly learned that *our* choices have to be always front and center in our thinking. And if not, we can surely end up seriously confused and painfully hurt – or for that matter, leave others seriously confused and often painfully hurt. It is the Kabbalah way. And like I said in the beginning, funny enough, it was Madonna who introduced me to this path. This was Irony at its best.

I've had other teachings over the years, as well, that offer a similar message. They're all just packaged up differently. Vipassanna, the ten-day silent meditation process I went through, teaches that through one to two hour meditation sits, and through basically depriving one of the regular everyday personal interactions we are accustomed to – like looking to another for a response, or validation, to support us with our position on a certain point of view; and everyday practices like reading, writing, talking on the phone, and even exercising – the student can arrive at a deeper investigation into how he thinks, and how he chooses, less outside interferences.

The individual develops a more *conscious* clarity

process, so that when one is up against obstacles, they can make more practical choices. My Religious Science studies – at the Agape International Spiritual Center in Los Angeles, taken over five intense twelve-week sessions – gave me very similar guidance, with their teachings emphasizing the responsibility relationship of your mind linked to that intangible omniscient force of creativity. All of these studies, despite their shell, fall again straight back to *you.* You the person, and your thinking. You the person, and your speaking. *You* the person, and *your* conscious choices.

Yes, I suppose, without that awareness, we might be served in being allowed to be webbed to our over-stuffed egos. But we are also kept in the maze of demands put on us by everything else around us. Which in the end, prevents us from being the brilliant, whatever-we-desire-to-be-person we so savagely scratch and claw to become. On the other hand, I do now see that, if we were to choose to step up and take the reins of responsibility – responsibility for what we have, responsibility for what we allow others to lay on us, and definitely responsibility for what we put out – we could gallop ourselves far away to a never-never-land, where joyful sighs envelope the soul. *Conscious choice living.* Oh, I like how *that* sounds.

The Dam Breaks

"'Carlton, I'm going to have to take you through your whole story a few times,' the detective explains to me. 'I'll have you tell it to me once or twice, and then we'll put you on tape.'

'Go.'

'When did it first happen? And where?' The detective asks me.

'My brother, Tony, and I studied karate at the local dojo during the summers when we would stay with our Aunt Rose. The very first time, Gary was taking my brother, Tony, and I on a trip to Disney World. We were coming back from the trip, and Tony fell asleep in the back seat.'

'I was in the front seat, sitting next to Gary. I remember him sliding his hand over and starting to touch my thigh as he was driving. That first day, that was pretty much all he did. He had that little hand thing happen. I was eight years old.'

'I was thinking, "But Tony is asleep in the back seat. What if he wakes up and sees us?" I don't know how I knew, but I understood that this was something that was supposed to be happening in secret. I guess it was by the slowness of his hand. It felt different than when he'd slap me on the shoulder and say, "Hey, Carlton, how are you doing?" There was something mysterious in the way he was touching me. It was creepy crawly, like a spider inching toward your leg.'

'We got back to where Gary was house-sitting for this family who was out of town. He takes Tony into the other room and puts him to bed or something.'

'There were oranges in a bowl. I was waiting in the living room, feeling that dead time when the quiet house is about to be filled with someone. I remember him using the oranges in that bowl as the initial lure.'

'Tony was sleeping upstairs and Gary comes downstairs.'

'He asks me, Do I want anything? Maybe

an orange? He takes the bowl of oranges out by the pool, and it is there, out by the pool, that the whole thing really gets started.'

'Gary had a certain kind of smell, a bizarre and sour smell I'd never smelled on anyone else. And the oranges were another smell. To this day, every time I see a bowl of oranges, or smell oranges, I remember.'

'That day was all about me touching him. It was always about me gratifying him. It was never the other way around.'

'He's sitting on a lawn chair, and he has on blue gym coach shorts. I remember him sitting on that chaise lounge in those shorts. I sort of walk over, see him peeling an orange. He offers me some, looks out at the pool. He lays back.'

'"Carlton, here, sit next to me." He slowly places my hand on his leg.'

'His thigh felt hairy. He unzips his shorts. I'm beginning to touch him. I have the strange sensation that I am under a microscope, like everything is being watched and noticed. It all seems like it must be very obvious to everyone what is happening. I have the sensation of cameras being around.'

'"My brother is probably looking around the corner," I'm thinking. "I just can't see him."'

'Nobody was supposed to be seeing us, but I knew better. "Someone is seeing us," I thought. "Someone is going to find us and we are going to get caught. I am going to get in a lot of trouble."'

'I just knew that, at any minute, Tony was going to come around the corner.'

'It seemed so secretive, what was happening, so exaggeratedly disguised, that it must have been terribly obvious. To this day, any time something is supposed to be such a big secret, it never is. Things can't really be hidden.'

Several years ago, I had a partner, and I went to visit him at his house where he lived with a female roommate. I always wanted to do it in a way we could sort of be caught. For example, I wanted to play around in the kitchen, knowing the roommate was in the living room. Or if she was in the bathroom, I'd want to play around on the sofa.

'Why can't we ever have sex lovingly in the bedroom, like normal?' He asked me. We got into a fight over it.

'Like normal? That's not exciting,' I thought. I always want to do it where it felt like there was some suspense goin' on."

Fireworks exuding rainbow explosions for the sky, and orchestras preaching triumph. These are expressions for the kind of super Fourth of July holiday that binds us to a time of liberation.

That is *not* where I was at in the summer of 1993, when a series of events had me feeling anything but liberated. Those events revealed me wrapped in a flag of fear and serious manipulation, rolling me tighter and tighter into a web of unfortunate deception. Before I tell you my story, I want to share some thoughts about manipulation and deception.

Even though I love the sun with all its sparkle and its magnetizing splendor, I sometimes wish it could be midnight gloomy and rainy outdoors. That would give me an excuse to hibernate, so to speak, and not have to deal with anyone – or at least an excuse to show up for daily activities in my dark and slippery way and blame it on the weather. It's all about finding ways to give myself permission to do what I feel I need to do. A grammar school teacher once told me that if I have something difficult or challenging to do or say to someone, I should do it when I'm tired, and that way I will be the most honest about the situation and will not edit the truth from myself.

Now, from a purely selfish point of view, my cleverly calculated choices can seem to make absolute sense. But when I look at them all a bit deeper, I realize that something gets in the way, and that is the *selfish* aspect of the equation. I know that life can get real difficult for all of us at times. And we all should be setting boundaries so that we can maneuver ourselves efficiently around the difficult people, and the circumstances they bring us – especially as we strive to survive inside our dog-eat-dog society.

But when I look at the end result of our *me* for *me* manipulations, I see that yes, we might walk away feeling proud of how we've handled someone, or dismissed someone for that matter. But what falls into my lap is the question of "Have we been the most responsible for that other person – that other divine entity that was established by GOD?" I know, for myself, the answer more times than not, has been a loud and glaring NO.

In the piece of poetry that opens this book, I ask myself the question, "When did what I thought become so insignificant to me?" But today, I pose a different question. "How have other people's feelings become so insignificant to all of us as a society?" With all the media coverage of celebrity misfortunes, like those of O.J., Michael Jackson, Robert Blake, or even Paris Hilton, that seem to beckon us into unabashed gossip and finger-pointing, it seems like it's become an almost celebrated invitation to just blurt out whatever, about whomever, whenever, with no personal consequences.

But what I've learned over time from my own foolish callousness is that we induce the silent sufferings of our lives, far more than we are aware. This brings me to the arena of Responsibility. Since we presently have a society with a growing acceptance of the "all-as-one" spiritual concept, how can we *now* actually sit comfortably knowing we are throwing poisonous daggers, causing other human beings to run desperately into hiding, as if they were leprous second class citizens? How could this still be going on today? And I won't even bring up the whole reality TV frenzy of, "Let's lift 'em up so we can laugh at them" thing. It's all just too insane for words.

I believe accessing all situations from the heart with Responsibility is the greatest act of love we can ever offer. Responsibility equals caring. So, as we investigate the choices we make in relationship to others, let's ask ourselves, if we are all really more prepared today to accept our oneness reality, wouldn't it be a better party for all of us if we left our weapons at the door?

At the end of the day, who's to say what truly keeps us from reaching the premium heights that we desire? What keeps us from the healings and the financial security? And the abundance of liquid love? Could it possibly be because we haven't shown up to our daily affairs chock full of heart grace for another? I suppose the only way to really know if our seemingly invisible choices are truly keeping our own lives in a static position or not would be to step out on a limb, turn up the heat, and eat life from a cleaner plate. *And then compare the results.*

Anyway, the series of events I was about to share with you began at Madonna's home. The thick textures of beautiful silk fabrics in hues of gold and blue creating her softer furniture pieces, the other rich dark wood chairs and tables, the fragrance of gardenias and tuberose swelling from every corner, as well as the mellow old sounds of Marvin Gaye flowing into heavy underground house music – all this became the glue that so engaged me in a much anticipated time for celebration.

Even in her home space, Madonna has a way of combining the elegant with the casual and edgy like I've never experienced with any other celebrity. On this particular party day, there were probably only about twelve guests there. She kept most of her home-frolicking affairs fairly intimate, with the guests being a potpourri of personal friends mixed with famous musicians, actors and actresses. Her guests included the likes of Willem Dafoe, Flea from the Red Hot Chili Peppers, and Diane Keaton. My attention fell more fully upon a less public figure, a Latin Adonis – I'll call him Mr. X. My experience with him is one *I will never – and should never – forget.*

That holiday party was a blast. We all meandered around, trying to appear very interested in each other, while the truth, as I believe it, was that we were all just waiting our turn to bask in the charm of Madonna herself. After throwing back many margaritas and glasses of red wine, the dancing, laughing, visiting with old familiar friends, and flirting, all seemed to reach their own sublime crescendo – which I suppose, is what released my courage enough for me to step up to that olive skinned beauty of a man I had been eyeballing.

Yes, throughout the day, we had both been checking each other out, but only in and around other people's short, trivial conversations. He and I never had any substantial, focused talk time of our own. I was becoming impatient, and figured I should do something about it. But I wanted to wait for the time when no one else was surrounding him. I could tell he wanted to be discreet. Once that moment arrived – that window of opportunity – I slid right in, went right up to him to make my move, and dug a bit deeper.

As I did, he said, "Oh, I'm gettin' ready to leave." He then slowly angled the final drips from his drink into his mouth, his eyes staring right into me, saying, "Why don't you do the same?" I was instantly numbed. Not a word came out of his mouth. Not a single word. It was only his eyes speaking to me – speaking absolute lust. And I got the message quick and clear. Oh yeah, I knew how to do that game well.

So, I instantly eased myself away from him and began, just as he did, to give my farewells to all the other festivity partakers. Separately, we moved through Madonna's house, from the white-cabinet-chrome-appliance-kitchen, through the stark grass-laden garden, to the pool hosting scantily clothed bodies. We were slicing our way around fast, preparing for our exit. We were destined for a different kind of socializing.

He was at the party with his best friend, but I realized he was preparing to leave alone. So, I gauged my goodbyes so that we would both end up walking out at the same time.

Once we did eventually clear past everyone and make our way out the front door, he said, in a continuing stride down the driveway, "My name is… Follow me." My heart began to race, so much so that it forced me to slow down my walk a bit, to take in the gravity of what was about to happen. I said nothing. He said nothing else. I simply did as requested, and we were on our way.

We made our way back to his apartment, and opened our talk time with how we had both recognized each other from the Fourth of July party Lady M had hosted the previous year. Our time spent was very delicate. He shared how he had been thinking of me since the year before, and how he had wanted to get with me back then, but was too insecure because he hadn't been with guys yet. Of course, I was extremely flattered. He was masculine, sexy as hell, hadn't been on the scene for long, and was interested in me. What free-spirited man in his right man would not have been thrilled? This all got me so stirred up. For me, the only problem standing in the way was my diagnosis information – and how I was in hiding about it.

With the reality that he was new to the whole man-to-man thing, I knew I should really step up to this one differently. Also, I knew that his best friend was a good friend of Madonna's – the icon that was helping me live out my dreams – and I knew I couldn't afford to jeopardize my position with the pop diva. *So you would think I would have walked immediately away.* But I did not. I was torn, *oh so torn.* I knew what the right decision should have been, but my horny selfishness was getting the best of me – and it eventually won out.

Though I was feeling all hot inside for him, and he was ready to make a move that night, I knew I just couldn't. I knew I had to pull back the reins and pull them fast. But I was invested in getting to know him a bit further.

I chose for us to just talk for the rest of the night, sharing about mundane things – typical first date stuff. "I'm from... my family is... I moved here in..." All the blah, blah, blah stuff. We wrapped up our time together somewhere around 3:00 in the morning. We exchanged numbers and said we would talk soon. And then I left. Nothing sexual happened then at all. Nothing.

It was all so mysterious, and I couldn't believe I was on my way, driving home alone once again. I was frustrated, excited, and nervous, all at the same time. I debated and debated with myself for a whole week, and then I decided I was going to do it. I was going to call him, and dive all the way in to have him as mine. And I did just that. I used all the charm and wit that I could, and he fell for it, all of it, exactly as I had hoped. Yes, Mr. X and I were officially happening, but in a matter of a few weeks, sadness and strife swarmed swiftly in.

It was such a wild ride with him. We spent much time liquoring it up – Vodka or Margaritas were our main picks. We drank a lot and laughed, which eventually led to us rolling around in bed a bunch. Then, we drank too much and fought. Our sex time definitely played itself out around both of those extremes of behavior, which of course always led to me feeling deeper pangs of guilt.

Mr. X was a different man for me. Not only was he a trust fund baby, and seemingly proud of it, he also seemed to be so into the whole Madonna thing, that oftentimes he felt more like a fan than a partner. It was strange. But my bizarre hunger for validation kept me in the mix. Mr. X was always so eager to hear about what went on at the gigs, so I kept him distracted with my career, and the ins and outs of the tour. That way, I could avoid the more serious issue of my deception.

I remember telling him about one particular incident – a very special moment with Madonna that was a real eye opener, even for me. This was a "Girlie Show" sound stage moment. We were in the last three weeks of the rehearsal process. In those final weeks of what was a nine week process, we would do grueling twelve hour days from 10:00 in the morning until 10:00 at night, with full run-throughs of the show twice a day, once at 5:00 p.m. and the final one at 8:00 p.m.

Starting at about 3:00 p.m., we would begin getting into full make-up and costumes. That way, Madonna could make sure the lighting and all of the other stage effects were exactly as they needed to be. I remember being off to the side that day, going over some of the steps for the show, while Madonna was still sitting in her chair, having her make-up put on. (There was one make-up person for Madonna and one for the dancers and the back-up singers.) As I stopped for a second to take a glance at what was going on with the leader of the pack, her make-up artist hesitated for a moment for Madonna to check out how her show face was coming together. Madonna leaned forward in her chair, her posture got all lifted up, and she began piercing right into the center of her beauty.

Her neck became pulled like a perfectly proud peacock, and her eyes became this glowing, magnetic, sunshine-magnifying glass, beaming onto the blend of the colors on her skin – the arch of her eyebrows, the slant of her cheekbones and the curve of her lips. It was like she was looking through a tightly focused lens at an image that was being acutely examined and prepared for editing.

Right then and there, the enormous celebrity we know her to be came fully into form. Time seemed to fold into a full freeze moment, except for a quiet rumbling of slow motion flash bulbs going off to catch her in her glory. Then, just as fast as that zoomed-in High Performance Diva persona of hers kicked in, I found myself standing with my eyes locked wide open with no dream reality happening at all. *Nothing at all.* As quickly as the vision overtook me, it had ended, and what was left was simply Madonna checking her make-up with noisy distractions all around.

I was like, "Holy shit! That was amazing. How did that just happen?" I couldn't believe how powerful that whole scene became. It was truly something to witness. That immediate super-celebrity transformation was a moment to remember. It was an experience that left even me feeling like a bit of a fan. I actually really enjoyed sharing that story with my Mr. X.

He was falling harder for me, while I was falling deeper into my pit of lies. He even went so far as to ask me a couple of times what my HIV status was, and of course, I said I was negative. While I did feel horrible saying that, I was comforting myself by at least making sure we always used condoms. I knew I didn't have any pre-cum and neither did he, so I figured we were both being as safe as we needed to be in that way. I also made sure that if I ever had a scrape on my knees from dancing, or a slight scratch on any part of my body, I would cover it right up before we had much contact. In that way, I felt like I was looking out for him as best I could. But deep down, I knew that the way I was going about it was not fair, because I still was giving him no chance to decide for himself what he considered safe – or unsafe. It was wrong and I knew it, but I was *so lost* – lost to shame, lost to fear, and lost to needing validation.

It was such an odd mixture of emotions for me. I couldn't seem to pull away from him, but I also couldn't find the strength to tell him my truth. We fought all the time, mainly because I was trying to get us to break up, but when it seemed like it might happen, then I couldn't seem to allow it to be. I was in and out of crying all the time. I would break into tears while we were out to dinner, first thing in the morning, and especially many times after we had sex, but Mr. X just had no clue as to why. He would ask me time after time what was wrong, but I couldn't muster up the strength to be real with him. It was a true love-hate concoction for me. This thing with Mr. X that I wished could have been a relationship anchored in rich heart feelings was only a river of sadness going ghastly downstream.

I even remember going into rehearsal one day for the tour, and as Madonna came in, I said hello to her in a somewhat flirty way, which was fairly usual for a lot of us. But this day, she turned to me and said something so cold, I was absolutely stunned. I couldn't believe she had said something like that to me. This time, she wasn't doing her playful abrasive thing. No, this was a *real dagger*, and hurt me it did for sure. There was another dancer standing right next to me as she spoke, and he looked just as thrown by the statement as I. Exactly what led her to say what she said to me, I will never know. But it did let me know that Mr. X had probably been getting some private protective words from her.

Somehow Mr. X and I made it through the months of rehearsal in Los Angeles. Surely I would be able to cut it off once I hit the road, I was thinking. Our first stop was overseas to the awesome city of London. Back then, Madonna always chartered private jets for us. We had our private chef on board, with our custom drinks prepared to be placed in our hands as we finished our final steps onto the luxury airliner. We even had individual VCR machines in each of our seats, prepared to play whatever movie each of us wanted. Yes, it was an incredible time, but I could not frivolously enjoy it all, because I was too bogged down by the more personal baggage that was accompanying me on the flight.

I did manage to avoid Mr. X's phone calls for the first couple of days out on the road, but one day after breakfast, as I rushed for a shower before going out shopping, the phone rang. I thought it was another dancer calling to check on my timeline for leaving, but the voice on the other end was the tropical beauty I was trying to dodge. We talked for a few minutes and I remember hating the fact that I was beginning to grow such feelings of missing him. Though I had found some breathing space from my predicament, I was instantly caught in my trap again.

We spoke on the phone for a couple more days, then one night after feeling true thickening love for him, I got completely swept away by the sweetness of his voice, and stupidly decided right then to invite him to meet me at our next destination – Paris, France. How crazy was that? I am going to the land of romance and I'm planning for Mr. X to meet me there. Right then, I knew that this love battle was reaching a dangerous peak. I also knew that having him meet me in Paris was the last thing I should have been doing – especially if I really wanted this thing with him to be cut off.

Anyway, we made it happen. He showed up. And like a fitting storybook Parisian romance, we carried on. We ate adoringly at quaint outside cafes. We held hands as we walked inquisitively through the rooms of the Louvre Museum. The rainy days also coerced us into an even richer connection. And I discovered – thanks to much embarrassing teasing at the sound check the next day – that our Eighteenth Century Hotel Courtyard had cascaded echoes of our man to man feedings the night before, loud enough for everyone to hear. All of this was feeling so good, and so bad, all at the same time. Needless to say, by the time he left, no space for separation had been created at all.

At that point, I still had two more months to go on the road, and just like with all my previous relationships, I went right into my sabotage game. Mr. X would call and call, but I was clear that if my mission was to box him out, I should give him no time at all. So, I continued on with my dodging and darting for the remaining duration of the tour. I decided to lock my attention on the task at hand – being on the road. Amsterdam – working up a frenzy for all the worshipping fans. Istanbul – racing through the streets, trying to find the best deals on the rugs and the Moroccan glassware. Sao Paulo, Brazil – fighting off crazy fans that were scratching and clawing to yank me out of taxis as I tried to make it out to dinner.

I did all of this while trying to make sure I was tending to my health the right way. Because from country to country, and city to city, I was performing outside against completely different climates, while most of the time wearing little to nothing onstage. And though, to the naked eye, I was wholly stable in my health, I knew the truth. *I had been diagnosed Positive and at that point, was not on meds.* And neither my T-cell, nor my viral load count, was in a balanced position, so I really knew I had to keep my focus. That included not letting the strain of the whole Mr. X situation take up any more space in my mind at all. I truly could afford no additional stress. Anyway, even while knowing what I had gotten myself into, I had the strong sense that my body would show itself as an iron machine, and get me through okay. And luckily, my prophecy proved correct, because, by the end, I made it all the way home with no complications – *no health complications, anyway.*

Once I was back in Los Angeles, I found I just couldn't get Mr. X off my mind. A couple of weeks went by, and I managed to not contact him, and he never reached out for me either. So I figured he finally got the signal. For me, this was a good thing, a necessary thing. But, just as always, Mr. X broke the no-call drought, phoned up, and seduced me into seeing him.

I truly believe it was God's work at hand, to begin the process that would finally stop me from playing the twisted game in which I found myself tangled.

Mr. X and I got together twice within my third week back, and the second time, although I told myself I would not have sex with him, I fell right back into our messy web. This time, I was absolutely disgusted with myself. I couldn't believe I was truly that weak. That moment for me was like a terrifying police siren screaming up behind me, demanding me to stop my motion or else. *This warning was loud and it was clear. I knew I didn't want to continue doing what I was doing. No matter how careful I was being, I was still running the slight risk that he might contract the virus from me, and that would leave me handcuffed and imprisoned to mourning for life.* So, I buckled down and decided I was absolutely going to finally tell him the truth of what had been going on the whole time. *He did deserve that – at the very least.* He was only trying to love me. He was no criminal.

I called him up and made plans for the two of us to go for a drive through Griffith Park. I asked him to drive, thinking that if he became dangerously furious, justifiably wanting to harm me, I would be the one forced to hit the pavement for the long walk home. We made our way to the park and it was instantly feeling way too sweet and bonding, so with every degree of strength I could muster, I asked him to pull the car over, saying I had something I wanted to talk about. I'm sure he had no idea my bomb was about to be dropped. But the moment for truth had arrived.

I took a few slow breaths, tried to speak, paused for an

additional breath, then looked him straight in the eye *and began to confess to him my entire plotted course.* Initially, he just looked at me, somewhat blankly. I couldn't tell what he was thinking. Was he going to be sympathetic? Did he actually understand what I said? Was he about to faint? I really couldn't tell. Then, like a dam burst open by a ton of explosives, he went instantly into wailing and tears. He started screaming, "No…No…No," and his face became so twisted with rage. He jumped out of his Range Rover and started pacing around like a true madman. He seemed so broken and unstable, I thought seriously that he might try to drag me out of the car and beat me down to a bloody pulp.

Thankfully, he did not. He just kept screaming and pacing. Eventually, he got back inside the car, and to my enormous surprise, began to hug me. I was stunned. We both sat there, gripped to each other's sobbing. All I could think to say, over and over, was, "I'm sorry… I'm so sorry… I'm so very, very sorry." We continued locked together in our unified crumbling, I don't know for how long. And though it was a horrible scene, I knew right then and there that at least, I was finally set free.

Though of course Mr. X wanted nothing to do with me ever again on an intimate level, he did show much real concern for how I was managing physically, and how I was doing emotionally. I was indescribably grateful. We remained in contact for awhile, mainly just through talking on the phone, but within only a couple of months it was clear that, although Mr. X did really care for me, he really needed more space from me in order for him to digest all that he had gotten himself into. Eventually, he just stopped calling. And considering all the events that transpired in the time we shared together, how could I protest?

So, let's cut to about six months later. I am in New York, working on a play called *Blade to the Heat* at the Public Theater, for The New York Shakespeare Festival. I got a message on my cell phone from my dear friend Niki, saying she had a bone to pick with me, and to call her back. I couldn't understand what she could be talking about, so I rang her back to inquire. She immediately leaped right in to ask me why I hadn't told her that I was diagnosed Positive. Of course, that was the last thing I thought she'd be wanting to talk about. But there it was. I couldn't believe it, but I could surely hear the frustration in her voice. So, I then asked her how she had found out. My mind was working fast. I figured Fate must have come around, and that it had to have been from Madonna herself.

Not exactly. Niki proceeded to tell me that she was out at an intimate party, and she overheard someone in Madonna's inner circle – and you know who you are – telling everyone exactly what I had done to Mr. X. I paused for a few seconds, then tried to create some chatter about the whole thing. I don't remember what I said – I was too much in shock at the time. I'm surprised my heart didn't stop right then and there. Niki then said that she was so pissed at him for handling the whole thing the way he did. Then she said she loved me, and that nothing could ever change that. She said that she was only upset because I didn't trust her love enough to know that she would never turn against me because of the kind of health dilemma I was in.

While I did appreciate her support, once I got off the phone, I also realized that my Pandora's Box was now fully exposed – far surpassing the exclusivity of the Madonna camp itself. *Yes, my ultimate fear was in full bloom, and my secret was now circulating all around town.* The reality of that left me just devastated inside. It was then and there that my interest in love completely escaped me, and my severe hibernation kicked in.

I will say that the most upsetting aspect of the whole scenario was the fact that I fell into such darkness because I was narrow-minded about what and who I was. I gave myself no position of power whatsoever. I allowed the potentially pre-conceived conclusions of other people, and their deluge of gossip, to tie me into a knot. When I look back on all the years I've spent living that way, with so much shame, I feel such a deep sense of sorrow.

Love, for me, has been an inexorable quest, but thanks to my silent times induced by my concerns over my image, I had time to go deeper into the whole matter. And what I realized is that my lack of love wisdom was not at all because I was slow-brained or way too selfish. It was the addictive abuse syndrome that stemmed from my most formative years driving me, as an adult, to seek out relationships to fit familiar prototypes…

Prototypes like my dad – who was physically and emotionally abusive, and an addict to drinking. And my childhood karate instructor – the perpetrator of the molestation early in my life – who was an addict to sex. Both men were power figures for me, and with both men, I submitted to their intimidation so I could avoid being subjected to their rejection. I so desperately wanted their love. *For all these years, as a grown man trying to thrive, I have been playing things out like I did as a wounded kid.* That was a profound insight that came to me some thirty years later, thanks to my therapist.

My male lovers – Dan, Ken, and Mr. X, were all a perfect fit to this destructive pattern. I would rush right in to their degree of alcohol, marijuana, pills, powder, or sex use, while simultaneously squelching the truth of what I really wanted and who I really was. I remember so many days wanting to say no, but my fear of them judging me – or even worse, dismissing me – kept me in my lies. *This unrelenting degree of compromise, I thought, was what love was all about.*

When I look back on the fact that, starting at such a young age, I felt such a longing for love – at any expense – I see now that those early years of education about what it meant to love, and be loving, is what developed my mind to be like a knot, all twisted up. It was that equation of circumstances that was truly the culprit behind my confusing behavior and for that matter, it led to my being diagnosed Positive.

All of these circumstances have played into the wrath of irresponsibility that has circled my life for far too long. And *I am so very tired of it.* And to Mr. X, whom I ran into many years later, and learned that though he had not contracted HIV from me, his heart had been severely broken by me, I have to say, wherever you are today, *please, please, believe that I never meant to hurt you.*

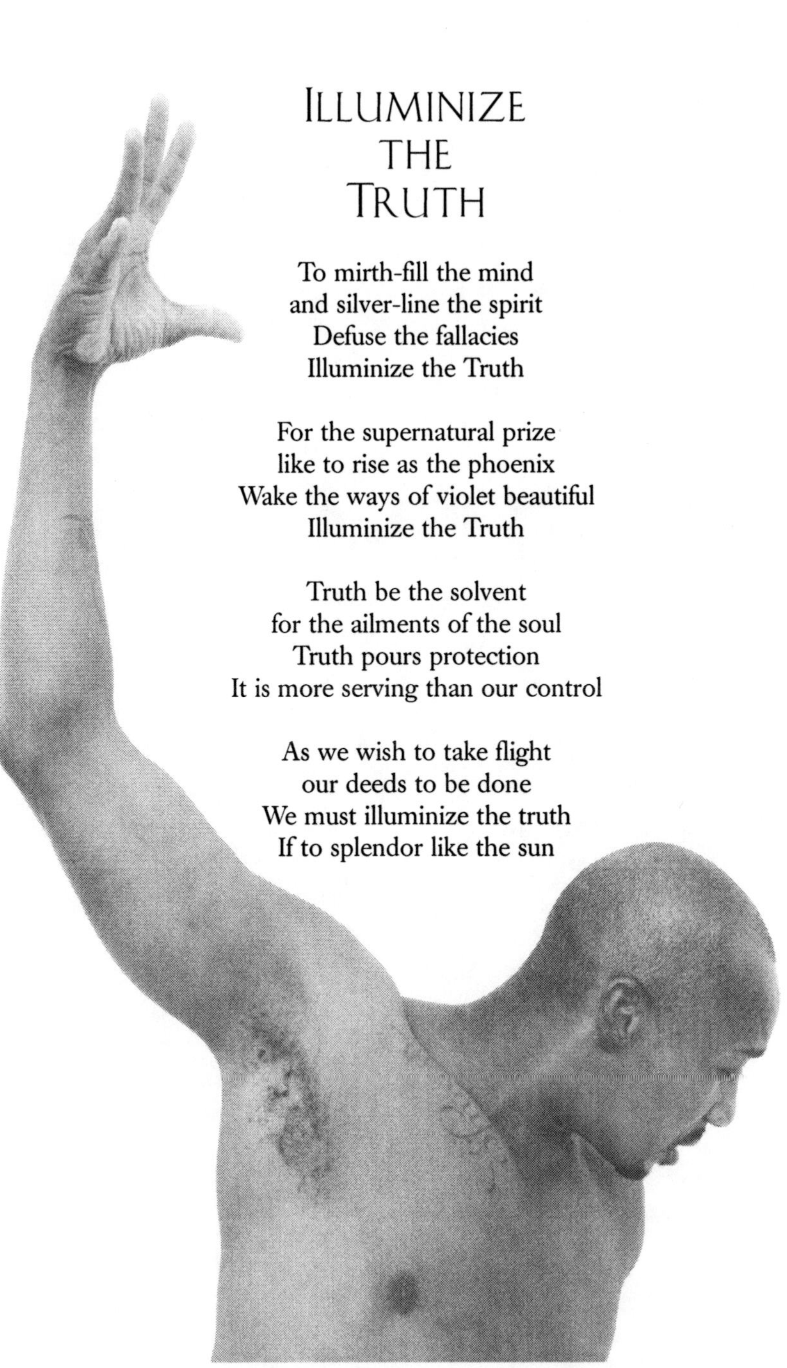

Illuminize the Truth

To mirth-fill the mind
and silver-line the spirit
Defuse the fallacies
Illuminize the Truth

For the supernatural prize
like to rise as the phoenix
Wake the ways of violet beautiful
Illuminize the Truth

Truth be the solvent
for the ailments of the soul
Truth pours protection
It is more serving than our control

As we wish to take flight
our deeds to be done
We must illuminize the truth
If to splendor like the sun

Being Heard

"By the time I was thirteen years old, Gary was married, with a three month old kid.

I had spent the day with Gary and ended up crashing at his place. I was asleep on the sofa bed in the living room, and somewhere about 2:00 or 2:30 in the morning, he comes in and wants me to do what we normally did – with me penetrating him.

That was the first time that the whole equation settled into being seriously wrong in my mind. Before then, he hadn't been married or had any kids. Plus, no one else had ever been so close by before when the real deal was going down.

He is on the sofa bed and I'm fucking

him. His wife is in the other room. And a little baby is in a bassinet.

I thought, 'This whole picture is really, really wrong.'

In the in-between years, when I was eleven or twelve years old, I remember one time I had spent the day with Gary. We had gone somewhere, and we were walking up the exterior stairs to his apartment.

He was wearing those little coach shorts again, and I knew we were going back to his apartment in Boca Raton to play around. That was par for the course for our relationship.

Everything was all relaxed and normal, and I was walking in front of him up the stairs. When we got closer to his door, he cut in front of me, and I smelled that sour smell again. It reminded me of when you go into an old person's house and it smells just like old skin. It doesn't smell like mildew, exactly, but it's a sour smell – almost dense.

That smell has no real life. It is a deadening smell.

Gary walks past me to his apartment door, and I smell that smell. That weird, deadening smell.

We go inside. We do our thing in the bedroom. We always used Vaseline. To this day, Vaseline feels extra edgy to me. I know I'm

about to do some serious shit if I'm using Vaseline. It feels much more animal-like.

I remember afterwards, lying on the bed, relaxed and talking.

'I hope you never get to the place,' he says to me, 'where every time a man touches you, you get turned on.'

What a strange thing to be saying to me, after he had created this whole thing with me that we did together. It was almost like a weird admittance from him that he was not settled with what he was doing. It did not seem like he was just trying to protect me from the way I was growing up, but that he was not comfortable in his own life.

Of course, there was never any telling me to use a condom. And while I didn't contract HIV directly from Gary, I did contract the habit of dishonoring my body and that of another person. And he reinforced that habit, time after time, with every single sexual encounter, summer after summer.

Being heard, and having your thoughts considered, is such a huge thing. I am specifically thinking about how I've been dealt with over the years by one very amazing man. I'm talking about Dr. Phillip Musikanth in Los Angeles, California. At the point of writing this, Dr. Phillip has been my HIV doctor for almost fifteen years, but he has always been more than my doctor. I consider him to be a very key element when I think about how and why my entire life has blossomed. His ability to listen to my needs and show up for me with an ear when I need it is more like what I would receive from a dear friend than what I would expect from a doctor.

Dr. Phillip and I came together after my initial doctor got fed up with the medical world, and decided to enter the entertainment industry. He is now a movie producer serving up some pretty cool projects, including "Twin Falls Idaho," one of my favorite films. It is a somewhat dark piece about conjoined male twins torn between their commitment to each other and their love for a beautiful vixen.

The emotional intricacies between the brothers are really worth tuning in to. One of them is seriously ill, and the depth of caring shown to him by his brother is so complete that it's as if it is his own life at stake. And of course, that is partly the case. Considering that they are linked together, each must rely largely on the other's well-being for their very own life. Dr. Phillip always exudes this same deep caring – as if his own life depended upon it. He makes me feel like I am not just a patient but a loved one.

Without a doubt, he is a truly-committed-to-his-craft kind of Western doctor, but that has never stopped him from considering, and often accepting the more alternative approaches to healing that I've introduced – and there have been many. Some were more challenging than others but nevertheless, he would usually give me the flag up without too much arm twisting.

One critical moment between us came when I brought a book to him written by a very controversial female writer. The book challenges the truths about what the epidemic actually is, and how it affects people. Basically, the writer takes the position that the virus, with its course of maintenance, is a scam to which *no one* should fall prey. I handed the book over to him, he opened to the introductory page, looked me hard in the eye, and then let out a soft breath of disappointment. His hazel blues eyes turned almost winter cold, and his usually inviting smile became instantly pierced with a nervous quiver. I mean, here I was, bringing in something that was stabbing directly at the world in which he had invested years upon years, not to mention who knows how much money for education. What should I have expected?

True to the character I knew him to possess, Phillip then smoothly adjusted his skeptical posture and began to strongly express his opinions. He never actually said that the position the book takes was bullshit. He did, though, as calmly as possible, make it clear that there was not enough substantiated evidence to support the data before him, and that I should be *very* careful. As he did so, I looked back at him with my eyes of defiance, and we moved instantly into much debate about what I thought and what I was intending to do.

The truth is that my decision had been made before I even got to his office. For me it was clear. *I was going to go off my meds.* I mean, they hadn't been giving us the results we wanted anyway. My numbers at the time – specifically my "viral load" count – was so out of range, it had actually surpassed the discernable range for an accurate detection reading. Still, I was convinced… *convinced* that the *reason* my body was rejecting all the drugs I had been trying, and had been for years, was *because it was a sign…* a sign that I shouldn't be on them at all.

He spoke. I spoke. He became intense. And so did I. We went on and on. The intensity of our heated conversation began to reach its tipping point, and it was right then that I realized I had to be very clear with him. I said, "Look, Phillip, I'll tell you straight out, if I go and do this and I realize things in my body are starting to get weird, then I'll come to you and we'll do something about it. I mean, believe me, *I'm not interested in living my life with things falling apart on me from one day to the next, either.*"

This time, he looked at me with a different kind of focus, and I also felt something different about myself in that moment. Then, in his usual heartwarming way, he sat straight up, and gave me a deeply compassionate look. We held each other's gaze for a long moment. In the end, he gave me the comforting "Yes" that I wanted – the green light to take charge of my own course of treatment.

The book I presented to him does indeed have fascinating theories, which were absolutely calling me to go deeper. And I did. I shared its ideas and ideals with my friends, searched online for more information, and began praying for more guidance. I don't remember how, exactly, but one rainy afternoon, I somehow found out that the author was going to be speaking that upcoming weekend. She was going to be at a center in West Hollywood, in a neighborhood not far from where I lived. I was looking to get greater clarity, and fast, and knowing that she was going to be in town was just the link I needed.

I juggled my already scheduled appointments, and made sure that I was available to show up to hear her speak. I was determined to dissect the whole thing, and go as far as I needed to go. I was so glad I did, for while the author did expound upon many powerful things, being there and seeing her in person also gave me some important information. Looking at her, I became aware that her physical well-being seemed a bit questionable. Her face sat curiously warped. Her should-have-been-porcelain skin gave off a murky hue. And there was something strange going on with the way she moved and walked around.

Were these conditions established from birth? Caused by some unfortunate accident? Or was something much more mysterious plaguing her – perhaps because of a strong denial, and unwillingness to comply with the medical assistance around her? I really couldn't put my finger on it. What I was clear about, however, was that with all the signs and information I had in front of me at that point, I had to make sure that I really lasered my focus so I could make the best of the personal decision I had so aggressively molded.

That moment in Dr. Musikanth's office truly became a character-defining moment for me. It showed me how I could take that part of me that I had always been proud to celebrate, that part of me that is able to stand face to face with all human confrontations without cowering, and channel it. My exchange with Dr. Phillip showed me how that part of me could serve me for something much grander than just the common volley of ego banter.

The whole incident with the book, even with the large looming questions that still surround it today, did prompt Phillip to say *"Yes"* to me, but more importantly, it prompted me to begin saying "*Yes*" to life. It didn't stop there, though. I began searching for all kinds of ways to get to the truth of what had happened to me, what might happen to me, and what I needed to do to supersede it.

I increased the number of massages I was getting. I refined my prayers. I started getting colonics. I did electrotherapy. I became more committed to acupuncture. I even took myself on a ten day silent meditation retreat. As I was writing this, I found myself at the beginning of one of the journeys that has also become a necessary ritual in my life – the glorious, most-of-the-time-challenging, always-and-forever-serving, *cleanse.*

This cleanse was for twenty-one days, but it was not actually that taxing. This cleanse is mainly about a modification diet, accompanied with a detoxifying powder, some added fiber, some flora, an herb that targets parasites and yeast buildup, as well as an herb that sends enzymes to the pancreas. That diet had me focusing primarily on vegetables and protein. Dairy, bread, pasta, caffeine, red meat, peanuts, all citrus fruits, and – funny enough – strawberries, were all excluded.

So, the first day I made myself some collard greens with

turkey meat (that's allowed) and baked chicken breasts. Of course, it would have been better if I could have added in some corn bread, potato salad, macaroni and cheese, and stuffing, but unfortunately, they were not on the menu. Oh well.

Believe me, I've had it far rougher than that. Over the years, I've done the apples-only cleanse for three days. I've done the dreaded olive oil/lemon juice CKLS (colon, kidney, liver, spleen) flush, which is done for one week with salads. But the most intense cleansing process was the ten day, liquid-only diet, consisting of two gallons of water a day, with lemons, cayenne pepper, and dark maple syrup. It's called the Master Cleanse. It also includes taking a laxative tea (as if you'd really need it on that cleanse) which, I must admit, had me in a tricky relationship with my sheets and the washing machine – not to mention the toilet.

While none of these cleanses were easy to maneuver, they did actually do the job. They allowed me to keep my body freer from the excessive build-up of toxins which comes from the repetitive drug regimens I had been on for over twenty years.

I am sure that this kind of conscious choosing on my part is one of the reasons my health has been so stable over the years. Sometimes I even question whether that super thin- skinned look of many diagnosed guys, and that protruding belly thing, might be because they are so congested with toxins. I have actually asked my doctor if most of his patients do cleanses, and he said "No." I then asked him if he thought it might help them, and he said, straight out,

"Yes." He even went so far as to say that he was going to start mentioning to his patients the concept of doing cleanses.

Dr. Phillip and I have such a cool relationship. He has always told me that my health situation is very different in that somehow, despite how crazy my numbers sometimes got, I remained very strong. He has said that it is probably because – in addition to doing my cleanses – I have dedicated so much time to things like meditating, speaking positively, and really going deeper in order to understand the source of my true power.

And I believe he is right. Yes – this path of looking such a crazed beast straight in the eye has been draining at times. But, I also know that it has made me stronger and wiser, and not just wiser about my health, but about my relationship with my creator.

Recently, I was driving in my car and I had a powerful wave of thought wash over me. The thought seemed vaguely familiar, but it had never struck me to that degree before. As the thought became more permeating, I tried to keep my focus on the usual – making the light adjustments of my steering wheel, checking the rear view mirror, staying aware of the others cars around me – but the insight that was scratching for my attention won out. I was forced to pull over and listen.

I was receiving a message about me being healthy. And about *God's* purpose for me. You see, thankfully, at that point in time, it was a solid twenty-one years since I had been diagnosed Positive. And after many failed attempts to truly balance my health – at least according to what was showing up on paper – something incredible had happened. A few days earlier, for the first time, I had gotten a phone call from my doctor's office telling me that *my viral load was now fully undetectable.* What that meant was that there was now *no activity of the virus in my body.*

How thrilled do you think I was? It's amazing how certain moments can freeze-frame your life for seconds at a time. That's what happened to me, thanks to that phone call. I sat there, parked on the side of the road, absorbing this obviously good news. At the same time, I was beginning to feel a bit strange inside. As I tracked my feelings, I realized that the duality of emotions inside of me was stirred up because of a feeling of disappointment. I was disappointed in myself for being so deeply affected by the numbers – even if this time, the numbers were good. Better than good – amazing.

You see, for survival's sake, during all those years that I was wrestling with my health, I had conditioned myself to believe that the continual frustrating results coming from the doctor's office did not matter to me. I had decided within myself that I was going to live my life with my badge of health based only on how I was feeling, and on nothing else. I could not afford to keep my attention on what the tests had to say about me. They kept saying that my health was weak. I had to force myself to believe that I was stronger than my test results – strong, no matter what the numbers said. I suppose that in that way – in being able to direct my attention beyond the challenge in front of me –

all my years of using my imagination to manifest what I wanted for dance, music, and acting paid off more than I thought.

I also see now that, living with my own beliefs – labeled by some as "Carlton's World" – which has, at times, made it difficult for others to deal with me for one reason or another, has benefited me greatly. Denial. Some say it has no place. I say it's not that black and white.

Let's return to my moment in the car. There I am, with my car pulled over, when I realize that the message coming to me is actually from my spirit talking to me. It was the voice of *God.* This Spirit Voice was saying, "It has never been in the cards for you to be taken out by this disease." It was saying, "This whole HIV journey of yours has been about you needing to build a relationship with *God*, so that through Him, you could prove His grace. You were sent through that valley of darkness to learn about the strength and the power that has been placed inside of you. Your path was decided so that you would come up against your own Goliath, and end up the conqueror. You were chosen to have this exact scenario in your life. It was to show you that by having an intimate relationship with The One Above, you can always be a winner." That message was loud and clear and it has never let me rest since.

Yes, it is so clear to me now. All along, it was not only Dr. Phillip taking heed of my needs, but the Big G Man as well. I see that every step of the way, all the desires I've had – to take on the many processes for healing and understanding – have been *God's* voice speaking through me, for me, as me... to hold me steady, build me up, and then carry me through to a more luscious garden reality. This Spirit voice, as my oldest sister Felecia told me, was leading me to step further into my Divine Purpose. She said that if I received such a powerful gift, and did not step up to the plate to work my purpose, it would be the most ungrateful thing I could ever do to God. That just sounded so right to me. And with that, I said to myself, "Okay, Carlton, it's time. Dig in, Dude." And to the rest of the world, I said, "Catch my wave of dust if you can, 'cause off I go."

I said earlier that one of my biggest lessons about my own personal power came from being heard. And now I realize that the flip side of being heard is listening. The decision to go off my meds when I did, the support I received when Dr. Phillip really got my need to do that, my ability to stand up in the face of fear, state my truth, and make my decision no matter what anyone thought – all of that was about *being heard.*

As I said, the other side of that coin for me is listening – *truly listening.* To the voice of God inside of me, and the guidance it's giving me. After going off meds for awhile, and allowing my body to detoxify, I felt guided to go back on the protocol – which I am on today. And I know that whatever goes down in my life, as long as I stay tuned in, and go deep enough to truly listen, I will be guided to the best choices for me at every step along the way. Listening is as important for saving my life as being heard. It's all about balance.

Honey Dispenser

"There are many things about being with Gary that I don't even remember. Like how Tony and I ended up taking karate classes. I only know that suddenly we were with Gary – and that he was the son of my Aunt Rose's boyfriend. I remember that Gary used to play golf, and I remember going with him to Disney World that first time it happened when he touched me in the car. I don't remember who set up that trip to Disney World.

I also remember that when I was eleven years old, Gary came by the house one day to pick me up, and brought me a stack of twelve

> to fifteen different straight porno magazines. They were full-on, extremely graphic ones, beyond Triple-X rating, mainly images of young women spreading their stuff right to the camera. I would later find out from the detectives that this was the stuff guys like Gary would use to back up their defense if anything ever came out.
>
> They could say, 'Oh, no, I'm innocent. I encouraged his heterosexuality.'
>
> Getting those porno magazines was a big deal for me. That was the first time I ever masturbated, and I had my first orgasm to one of those magazines. When that crazy relief came for the first time, I wasn't sure if something was wrong with me. All I knew was that now I had that stack of magazines I could use all the time.
>
> Between my time with Gary, and the explicit magazines, I learned to become completely focused on someone's sexual opening – without it ever really being about me dealing with a guy or a girl…

It was 1996 when Honey Dispenser got his first TV Series Regular Role. It was just perfect – or so he thought. Honey Dispenser was playing a fireman – Ray Grimes, the tiller of the truck. He was thinking, "This is so awesome because, yes, it is a new show and all, but the character is *so straight."* He was most excited about that. *"Yeah,"* Honey Dispenser thought, *"everyone will view me as straight."* That's what was rolling through his head.

This kind of thinking just kept going… hiding, covering up, lies, and manipulations. Honey Dispenser was such a trip. The following season, he landed a recurring role on "Fame L.A." No, he was not dancing. Honey Dispenser was cast as The Film Director, with a beautiful girlfriend. "How great," he thought. Once again, everyone would think he was straight.

But, come on. Was Honey Dispenser *really* ever hiding anything? I mean, *come on.* He had done the "Blond Ambition" tour with Madonna only three years previous. And *Truth or Dare*, the documentary of that tour – sealed forever with truths – was released with moments and statements throughout that clearly separated him from the usual pocket of "let's fuck some pussy" boys.

Don't get me wrong. Honey Dispenser had his share of tongue-to-tits moments, but *come on now,* those were just moments. When he was growing up, Honey Dispenser had a lot more of that kind of action, but the full blown dick-to-muff-kind-of-guy-on-the-regular *Honey Dispenser was not. And he hated himself for it.* Honey Dispenser was not happy. How could he be when he was living his life dodging and darting? I guess ever since childhood, Honey Dispenser had been harnessing the same scared emotions and behaving in the same way. And the slam-you-to-the-ground comments which came from his dad about his sexual graces didn't help things at all.

So here was Honey Dispenser, trying to keep up with what everyone else hoped he was, instead of living out what he knew he himself to be. The fresh cellular canvas that was Honey Dispenser just wanted his father to love him. He did not want his alcohol-obsessed exit sign of a dad to school him about the touchy-feely dance like it was some sex motel scene. He just wanted his father to love him. He actually wanted *everyone* to love him, and didn't he try *everything he could* to get that to happen?

Honey Dispenser had always wondered why, when he was sixteen years old, his dad tried to teach him about the acts of sex. He recalled being about to go out on a date with this girl he really liked and telling his father about it. So, out of the blue, his dad proudly starts in with, "You know, you've gotta get that thing wet first. Make sure you get your hand down there and get that thing good and…" Honey Dispenser almost wanted to throw up. On the one hand, he was thinking, "What the fuck is this? Why is he talking to me about this stuff?" And on the other hand, Honey Dispenser is thinking, "Is he on to something? Has he figured out that girls aren't my main territory? Is he sensing something between me and Donald across the street?"

Either way, did his dad really think that was the way to go about it?

That ghetto-version TV room, with the aluminum foil holding the reception for the boob tube, the sloppy polyester sheets in a clump around the bed, that raggedy spaghetti-stained wife beater (and appropriate it was) t-shirt his father was wearing, his dad's unshaven face, bugged eyes, ashy leathered hands, the half-burned out bulbs from that fluorescent lighting – for Honey Dispenser, all of it just pissed him off.

So Honey Dispenser blurts out, "Dad, I don't need you to tell me that." Could his father have really believed that was brown sugar, saying that to him? He nipped that Tabasco effort right in the bud. Honey Dispenser did not want those nickel ideas from his dad. How could Honey Dispenser ever truly value himself when he had no real padlock to protect him from his own dad? He needed love, not this show-off-the-keychain bullshit.

So he decided he was going to get his love *somehow, some way.* And off he went – and he surely went off.

He was trying to become sugar scooper, cocoa-powder happy, with no red pepper on his path. But it was not pretty. He found himself up against suffering sweat, just waiting to be touched. There were feet curled into ragged sofas, and nakedness at foreign windows all the time. He even found himself holding hopeful steps as he salivated over alluring limbs down the lonely food aisles at the market.

All he remembers thinking was, *"Make me know I'm important."* His behavior was a collage of, "If I do your drugs, am I enough? If I drink your liquor, am I enough? If I let you fuck me unsafely, will that do it? How about if I let you ignore me?" Honey Dispenser was trying everything – trying to understand, trying to be patient, trying to be loving – and mostly just trying to clean up all that mess. He was nurturing very strange ways.

Through his course of searching, Honey Dispenser remembered Oprah's *O Magazine* and the column she calls "What I Know For Sure." He had followed the column for many months and apparently, it had served him greatly. In his awakening, what Honey Dispenser realized he "knew for sure" was that whenever he was searching for a bigger life – be it on camera, in the shopping malls, or down the roads of personal intimacy – he was truly just needing more love to his heart.

Now he knows for sure that the love he has been seeking has to start with him – *with loving himself first.* It is written that God wishes for us all to love ourselves correctly. And as Honey Dispenser understands that statement more and more, he realizes it requires him to be fully honest about who he truly is. If that means he is needing more delicate communication, or if it is him caring to adorn himself with things supposedly unfitting for his gender, or if it is him as a man desiring another man – *then that is what it is, and that he must express.*

For, when Honey Dispenser expresses the truth which comes from his heart, he will always get to experience more love. That love brings on more peace. And when that kind of love is dispensed from Honey Dispenser to *himself,* then it will surely be all good in the neighborhood.

Shake the Shame-Maker

"The first time I was ever with a girl was with my little girlfriend, Sakina. It was in the middle of the Gary years. I remember being in her parents' basement, right at the edge of the bar, on the floor, so anybody coming around the corner could see us. We were right there.

I remember another very secretive scenario with two girls in an alley – after the thing with Gary had ended. I was in the alley fucking one girl behind a garbage can while the other girl stood guard at the end of the alley to see if any cars were coming. Then the two girls would switch places.

The first time I remember being with a guy was with my neighbor, Donald, who lived across the street. It may have been during the Gary years. I hung out at his house, sometimes had dinner with his parents, went up to his room and played games.

Then we started playing around. The first time was in the back bedroom of my basement. Even though I was the younger one, I remember being more the leader of us getting into it. Donald had never done it before, but he was curious with me. I remember standing up and Donald lying on the sofa. It only happened a couple of times, and then he put an end to it.

Donald was two years older than I, and while we did do it on the down low, so to speak, it did have more care to it overall. We were real friends.

It is 11:10 pm. on February 8th, 2006. A Wednesday night. I'm now in Florida.

"I think we should do it now," he says. "You've gone over it. You're all warmed up. Let's do it now. All the stars seem to be lined up to make this great." To the ears of a much intimidated performer, this deluge of words might have been stacked up to coerce you onto a stage, so you might leave your long overdue mark on an audience waiting with bated breath, hoping to be overtaken by your unabashedly surrendered performance. But I am not that timid person and this was not that type of night… not that type of night at all.

The voice continues. "We've got the tape ready to roll, but before we actually go and do it, you need to really make sure you've got your confidence. I don't want to feel you coming off unsure about anything. It's not going to help you. Are you ready?" The pressure begins to mount now. I'm not resembling myself in this moment. In fact, my fragile emotions have me leaking something rickety. But before I allow them to morph into a cemented state, the Power Performer version of me bolts forward. I then leap up – surely and defiantly – and say "Okay… okay, let's do it. Let's make the call." And then off we go.

I proceed out the door, curving left and right, left again, then straight ahead, as we make our way to our next destination. I'm in my serious take charge mode. Nothing is going to stunt my power now. My head is high. My shoulders are pressed down. And my soul is only about winning this moment.

We arrive at the waiting room. The man escorting me files in. As I step inside, the weight of the moment really swells forward. I'm initially taken aback by the very narrow, incredibly tight space before me. I notice golden curtains masking every corner of the walls. And the lighting is all from fluorescent bulbs registering hauntingly bright. My gaze makes its way to the left and there in a lone corner is a single side table with a solo telephone on top. The hand linked to the earlier commanding voice reaches down and yanks up the handle of the phone. I give him Carlton's don't-fuck-with-me eyes and say "Hold on just a minute..." I need to further penetrate a moment of prayer and focus. But Mister Quick Fingers proceeds to dial, ignoring my request.

Yes, it is Detective Chapin, with a sneering smirk on his face, this Fingers-Voice master who then thrusts the telephone handle toward my chest. I apprehensively take the receiver into my hands. He turns to dims the lights, slides on a pair of headphones, takes a proud seat in a chrome-and-fake-leather, way-too-worn-out chair, and gestures for me to do the same. We're all accustomed to this kind of investigation scene – straight out of the movies.

Before I can settle into the comfort of my cushion seat, I hear the line begin to ring. I then press the talk device to my ear, as the ringing grows, and eventually becomes continuous ringing. There can be no turning back now. This has to happen. And this is about to be a moment to last a lifetime.

Before I go any further with all that, let me first start out by giving a gargantuan acknowledgement to my brother Anthony Wilborn, or Tony as we call him – the brother who, just two days before I left for my Florida excursion, also admitted to being manipulated into sly-as-a-fox, creepy crawler sexual behavior during our summer vacation visits to the orange juice capital. *Just as I had been.* My brother who was so dismantled and aloof from our family tree since my mom's passing, now produced words of great power and human elevation to serve me in this most monumental situation. His words had me so taken aback because they were not from the shady street thug mold of a man I grew up knowing him to be. No, someone very different presented himself to me for this bare bones cause. And because his words rang right from the pages of the Bible, I was holding them tightly in my hands, cherishing the new Jesus ambassadorship challenge he placed in front of me. Yes, I was ready.

The phone rings one final time, and then it's picked up. I hear a gentleman's voice. I sturdily start out saying, "May I speak to Gary, please?" The man says, "This is Gary." Right then my heart takes a gasp. "Gary, this is Carlton Wilborn, Aunt Rose's nephew." And without a glitch of space he says, "Oh, hi Carlton. How are you?" Now, the last time I saw or spoke to Gary, I was thirteen years old. I am forty-one now, so I did not expect him to have such assuredness of who I was. But he clearly did.

Now the Detective's earlier coaching takes a strong stance within me. And with my mind remembering all the nuanced tools-for-this-moment-of-communication that he placed before me, I begin the performance of my career, a real-life performance for entrapment.

I dive right in. "Gary… I wanted to contact you, because I've been having a hard time dealing with the things that happened between us when I was a child." He says, "Yeah… okay." I proceed. And this I have to do by the book, to make sure we can hold him to the charges I am presenting. I have to lay it straight out. "Gary, when I was eight and nine and ten years old, why did you, a twenty-six year old man, have me putting my penis inside your butt? Do you realize how much that's messed me up in my life?" His voice becomes somewhat dulled and removed, then he lets out an, "I know…I'm so sorry." There is no hesitation of admittance on his part whatsoever. I am shocked, but also utterly thrilled. This task instantly becomes much easier for me than I could have ever had suspected it would be.

The conversation continues down its long and arduous course. This is such a crazy scenario for me to see myself in – on the one hand, because finally being set free were all the anger, blame, and shame that had engulfed me for so long, and on the other, because I was forcing myself to come face to face with the new perspective of living that my brother was igniting in me.

On this day, the position my brother Tony had taken on the subject before I left for Florida was like a loud Sunday service bell banging out a message that was nothing short of wholehearted *forgiveness*. But, this forgiveness thing toward Gary…oh, this felt like a really hard one for me to get with. I mean, I believe it was Gary, with his pillaging behavior, who started me down my whole lack-of-self-honoring path. The path that contributed to my dark, desperate, searching for love and validation at any expense. The path that was clearly the culprit for all of my drugging, manipulating and over-sexing.

With all this going on, how could it not have played a part in my mind being warped about the ways of love? How could I have walked along the rich pastures of prosperity? While going to the amusement parks with him, while watching him play golf, as he taught Tony and me karate, Gary gave me "Yes, you're okay, don't you worry eyes." But they were no gift. He was a liar. This man had vowed himself to a loving wife while breeding harmful fire.

In this event of confrontation, I was allowing myself to finally deal with the source of my blots and blemishes, my internal battle zone. But in choosing to step up to this moment, *this shake the shackles of my shame-maker moment,* I was also being guided to bear down and offer deliverance to Gary himself.

Yes, I could have easily gone the route that was being coerced by several close to me who were intending to warm my heart – the route of sending him up the slam-the-metal-bars-shut river. Or, the route of bringing a "Damn you" diminishment to his bank account, or at least having him court-order marked and followed, like a fugitive racing off to the foothills. All of which could have been easily justified. But God was speaking a different way to me, as confirmed by my big brother. "It is not your job to be the controller or detective of this man Gary. Leave that to the Father above. It is only your job to live, offering relentless forgiveness to even those carving the most damaging journeys, as Jesus did."

Oh, this was such a very complicatedly serious situation.

Though this crazy shame-inducing web caused my voice to be stunted for years, could I actually muster up the strength now to do the righteous thing, so that both Gary and I could crawl out of that chastising cocoon?

Anyway, my Detective-guided cubicle call does all of its curious curving, and then eventually finishes, with all the information one could need to send a man of such depravity into a gloomy dungeon. But I still am not satisfied. I just really feel the need to meet Gary, eyeball to eyeball. I really feel that it will empower me, if I can now bring a hiding-behind-nothing-not-even-a-telephone posture to this man. And with that decision, I decide we should actually do it at his church – yes, he's actually been a practicing minister for several years. I wanted to do this with his wife present, so we could finally set this thing aright.

After tossing and turning throughout the shut-eye hours in the Motel 6 double bed that feels more like a twin bed to my big-bodied self, I gather myself to have a hearty breakfast; wardrobe myself into confidence, then quietly absorb the words of my Bible, saturating myself with strength for the situation before me. All the while I can feel my heart prompting my fingers to tightly cross, hoping that all my taking of morning walks with deep meditations in the previous nearly three months, and denying myself booze and marijuana for mental focus, will pay off, so that I can be at my *Black Power* best.

Once my rental car makes its final turn into the palm tree riddled strip mall parking lot of Gary's church, I am surprised to notice how small it actually is. I check the rear view mirror to make sure the energy around my face is relaxed, and then I proceed inside. I am stalled for a few moments at the front door by an associate of his, but then directed into the sanctuary, where Gary himself is waiting.

And there he stands, now looking much less to me like the Goliath demon I had given him rights to be. Seeing him standing there after so much anticipation, I feel cold. I feel guarded. I feel strangely matter-of-fact. *I am on a mission, and I feel able.*

He immediately makes some comment about how big I am now, and then he guides me into the church conference room.

I notice piles of videotapes and huge religious reference books stacked along shelves, as well as several plaques along the walls with God messages attached. The setting could not have been more supportive for what I was intending. His wife soon works herself into the room, we share light hellos, we all take our seats, and then off we go.

I begin with some meandering blasé conversations about his church. How large was the congregation? How long had he had it? Stuff like that. Then, we start falling into an oozing, uncomfortable silence spell, which Gary tries to quickly fill with his emergency apologies. But, I cut him right off saying "Gary, honestly, I'm not here for that. I am only here to let you know…" I couldn't believe I was about to say it. The moment was actually upon me. "…that I do actually forgive you and that I love you." Wow! I couldn't believe I did it. Those words actually rolled out of me much easier than I had expected.

As I say that to Gary, he begins to cry. I then impulsively feel increasing compassion growing for him, as I watch his wife remaining in an impeccably calm and pillar strength posture. And before I know it, we have ourselves fully maneuvering through all of the "I felt this... My family did this and that... It was so hard because...I realized I learned..." kind of acknowledgements.

As all this expressing is reaching a richer level, I myself then offer up for the three of us to hold hands and do a prayer together. It felt like a fantastically crazy choice, but I did say it.

Once that gets underway, we seem to slide into a whole new heart accessibility level, where we are literally delivering to each other encouraging words. And then from there, I feel the room quickly swirling with a force of spirit that was inducing a sensation of *big love* that was almost tangible. It was incredible. This was a degree of expressing I did not foresee. Yeah, I tell you, God was working his thing out.

During our prayer, Gary begins to prophesy about the dance/theater company I'm developing. Each of our hands began to grip the other with more care. I am letting out guttural sounds of support. His wife keeps saying, "Thank you Jesus. Thank you God." Gary then falls into speaking in tongues. *The room was just pulsing with appreciation.* It was so wild!

As we open our eyes, exhaling from that powerful moment, it is clear that a major shift of grace is underway for each one of us. Tears of joy are slowly being wiped away, just as delightful smiles are beginning to be passed around. Forgiveness had not only taken over the room, it had set the stage for acts of service that I know were nowhere close in any of our could-conjure think boxes.

Then the most wonderful of all things presents itself.

Gary, in regards to speaking about the size he prophetically envisions for my new career position, mentions that he himself has no desire for his own business to become any bigger than he already is. He says that he is not interested, unlike many other devout pastors, in being all blasted over the airways of the TV, or the radio for that matter. And in an instant, spirit rips right through me in Gary's favor. I said "Hold up... Gary, it is not your job to put a cap on how far God can use you to bless people. How do you know that God doesn't need you to be Large like that, so that you can have more visibility and gain more status, which would only support your mission of soul healing going further?" Gary's eyes become bug-eyed big, and I notice his wife sitting with a seriously proud grin, and I'm like, "What's going on? Why are you guys looking like that?"

He then admits to me that his wife had already been trying to convince him to step his ministry up. "I'll tell you honestly, Gary, I think you don't want to be out there like that," I say, "because you're afraid of people judging you." Then I go in even deeper, and say, "You can't place fear before God." He says that I am totally correct, that he had been concerned, because he didn't want anyone who knew about his sexual child abuse past to now see him up there like that, wearing this God cloak, and think that he was trying to hide behind it. His eyes swell with tears.

He continues on about when he hit rock bottom, admitting to having done five years of prison time for his offenses against children, and how it caused him to lose his high powered corporate executive position, along with his millionaire bank account status. Then he says, "I vowed to myself in prison that if God brought me through all that, I would only serve him, and I realized that I didn't want any of that other stuff. I mean if he took it all away, then it was not for me to have it, and I vowed that I would never desire it again. I don't want anything to be about me anymore. I just don't want it to be about me. That's what got me in trouble in the first place."

In that moment, I am witnessing a severely broken-spirited man. I say to him, "Good, then don't keep it about you. Give it all to Him. Gary, you don't have to answer to anyone. If people see you doing what you believe you are divinely called to do, then that's between you and your maker. It's not your job to make sure everyone knows why you do what you do, the way you do it. And trust me, if someone does try to ignite some negative thing against you, if your commitment to God is true, He will protect you and thwart anything coming your way. And another thing I've learned, myself, is that God doesn't give us a taste of a certain level of living, and take it away, just for it to be some type of twisted tease."

I then share with him about how I had my own fabulous blessings of my TV series and my leased house in the Hollywood Hills, and how it all got snatched away, as well. I said "I believe God allows us to experience all that stuff, because those levels are what He intends for us, but He will take it all away, and keep it from us, until we get our characters more right, and we get right with Him. Gary, you need to be in that millionaire living. But, you're right. Let it all be about Him. How do you think you can largely serve God, staying as small as you obviously are? If you could let yourself grow into a lot more, how amazing might it be if you actually came across someone in need – let's say, someone with no place to live – and you could step right up and purchase a brand new house for them. Tell me that wouldn't feel amazing? You know it would." He then said "Wow, I can't believe you just said that to me. I have never thought about it from that perspective before. Carlton. That's so incredible that you just gave me that insight. This is such a blessing for me."

In that moment, I am really feeling for him, but I am also thinking about how ironic the whole scenario is – that I was actually there, able to show up with so much care and true heartfelt interest in this man's well being, the man that was the source of so much of my pain.

Then, fully loaded with spirit-seducing force, I say, "Look, why don't we all just stop the craziness now, and choose to free ourselves from the past, and let this visit be a blessing for *The Celebration of a New Life?* Come on, let's just start right now. This is a call for each one of us to celebrate a new life. Let's start right now. All of our eyes lock onto one another, and I sense that each of us knows that profound grace is flooding itself in, for our deliverance.

I even tell Gary that I am in the process of putting together the funding package for my new company, and ask if he would be okay with me sending a copy of it to him once it is done, for him to pray over. He says he would love to pray over it, that he had already been offering that type of service to major corporations and businesses, and that it did really good things for them. And he says that it would be his honor.

From there, we all hug, exchange our telephone, address and Email information for future communication, and with a perfectly on-fire soul, I am out the door.

Our entire three-and-a-half-hour event did indeed become the most anointed time.

Now seeing the entire unfolding of all the pieces to that curious puzzle, I believe God sent me through all of my days and nights, and hours of spiritual and character development, so that I could show up for that scenario, truly ripe, to facilitate such a pivotal, mutually necessary, soul-serving intervention.

Because of my ability to deliver up that large scale forgiveness, I can now see that Gary was presented into my life, with all his baggage, not for me to end up damaged, but for me to be, at the end of the day, further expanded. I can see that, as long as I am able to release forgiveness to whomever, in relation to whatever, I can never, and will never again, be a victim. This was the empowerment I longed to have encoded onto my soul. Yes, today I now know myself to be a man not with a heart manipulating and scarred, but with a heart truly capable of surrendering large scale unconditional love. But I now know that it had to come about organically, from the inside, not by me forcing a face to face with Gary.

My new big brother, a new understanding, and my new

heart ability… Ain't that somethin'. Am I grateful for that entire sordid maze? You betcha!

WE ARE GIFTS

Tall   Dark or Light   Bamboo Thin
to Sweet Melon Bigger
Short with a Sway or Straight
WE all define the godly figure

From hair so Intimately Tight
to the Merrily Dancing Long
it's the place of pure acceptance
that for ALL we should belong

We are the gifts We are the gifts
We are the gifts that shine
So perfectly different
uniquely intended and sublime

As we revel in this truth
we bring a silence to the disgrace
That formed from
delusion and dishonor
THEY put the mask on the face

Hamster Man

"Even at that young age, there was part of me that understood that what I was doing with Gary would allow me to have something over the other kids my age.

I grew up in the city, and that was about being street smart. When I was in Florida doing my thing with Gary, I would be thinking, 'Boy, when I get back to Chicago, I can talk about sex in front of all my friends, and tell them I learned how to do this and that. They don't have to know it was with a man.'

A part of me was into that aspect of it. Another part of me was scared and coming from a place of hiding. I liked that exclusivity, that secret kind of living. It empowered me in a certain way.

In a weird way, all the hiding I had to do with Gary allowed me to have something of my own. In my family dynamic, there was so much going on in my household that was exposed. Everyone was always there, always around, coming into your room, screaming, opening your door. I had no privacy at all.

Being with Gary allowed me to have something that was just mine. No one could take it from me. Everything in my family felt intrusive. But this thing I had with Gary was something no one could invade. I felt like I had something no one else could have a say in, and it made me feel more grown up, more mature. The fact that I had something I had to hold in gave me a bit of superiority from a place of grownup-ness.

My parents were very vocal about the things between them that bothered them, and about their issues, and they were sitting on a lot of ugly behavior. I felt like with Gary, I had some kinship to that.

I watched both my Mom and my Dad have secrets. My Mom had her boyfriends and her bank accounts and her very private lifestyle. My Dad had his other women and that was very private. So there was a certain

part of me that started to realize I had secrets too, and that allowed me to feel like I was more connected to my parents, in comparison to my peers. While this business of having secrets was a lot to deal with, I also had one up on my peers.

I was never really the kid that was accepted by everybody. I was skinny, small, and always felt taken advantage of and not appreciated very much. My feeling was, 'I have this secret life, so even if you don't approve of me, in some twisted way, I've got something you don't have, something better than you.'

The first time I remember being accepted into the hip crowd was when I started smoking pot with a clan of kids when I was fourteen years old."

I've been such the student in my life. In fact, I happen to have recently completed a class – an Image Marketing class. In the class, we were led through a series of exercises designed to give us deeper insight into what essence or message we put out to the world, so as to further nurture It for ourselves. This process was recorded on video for each student to take home and study, if we chose to do so, and you better believe I was a student that was prepared to do just that. To get a chance to see myself not as I wanted to be seen, but for *what I truly was,* with no Carlton spin on it – well, I was all propped and ready for that kind of revealing.

In the class, each student is asked all types of random questions – from family stuff, to food stuff, to how you feel about animals – and then asked some even weirder things. Some topics were fairly deep while others were just, as I like to say, more "curious." Nonetheless, each of them was revealing. I got all kinds of terms and statements thrown out about me, some of which I liked, and others that were more like having your diamond ring tossed in the mud, but in any case, they did all teach me a lot.

Whether I was perceived as confident or analytical, stylish, warm, aristocratic, insecure, headstrong, moody, caring, controlling, alluring or driven, I guess the point the class was there to make was this: all of us are complex individuals exuding far more information than we ever fully realize. And our job is not so much about adjusting ourselves to fit in, as it is about having a useful understanding of ourselves. And with that insight, we can use those outside perceptions of us simply to serve our goals – and find new ways to look at old words or phrases, so that we can be the best distinctive person we were designed to be. And if there's a little extra sugar to our character or even some salt, *we are what we are and it should all be fully celebrated.*

Yes, you can hold an orange in your hand and call it a ball, or paint it to resemble something else that's round. And you can even mold things around it so that it appears as maybe a snowman, but when you squeeze an orange, you will not get some creamy molasses syrup, you will get orange juice – 'cause that is the truth of the orange, whether you like it or not. I only wish I had gotten this lesson further back in my years so I didn't have to take myself through so much internal struggle, trying to make excuses for who I was, or better than that, *who I am.*

Towards the end of this tell-all twelve week excursion, I began to think about the three sessions of cosmetic surgery I'd gone through. They just came screaming back at me. You see, when I was about nine years old, some kids from my old neighborhood kept calling me this certain name, a name that I grew to truly *hate.* I don't like to use that "H" word, but that was my feeling. The word stung so bad I never wanted to be connected to it at all. The word was "Jibs." I never learned what it really meant, but I understood it to mean Ugly Fat Face – fat like a hamster whose cheeks are full to capacity with more than enough gravel food to feed a whole rodent family for a week.

The truth is that I did have a fairly round face, but I never thought it was a bad thing. That is, not until I started listening to the comments from those mean-spirited children. I never seemed to be able to get comfortable being judged by them, especially not in that way. And, for some reason, as time slid along, I chose to buy into their judgment, hook, line, and sinker, and I began to hate myself as well. I became so obsessive about my image that I was like a deranged child on Easter afternoon, hunting for the last of the speckled hidden eggs. Sadly for me, I was scouting for self-sabotaging mirrors at my every left and right turn.

But remember now, I did say I went under the knife

three times. And by the time that final session rolled around, my surgeon had become so frustrated with my nit-picking and my all too savvy attempts to change even *his* mind about what I looked like, that he began to tell me that if I went under again, it could be risky. Apparently, at that point, there wasn't enough fat to take any more out.

Now don't get me wrong, I was *not* the image of some circus freak with a cauliflower bubble-head, or someone with a face that should only be appreciated in dim light. Still, I did think I was somewhat off balance in the face area. So, I figured if I could erase the chances of being called essentially Hamster Man for the rest of my life, I was going to do so – and, I suppose, do so at any expense. It was my third visit with that insidious liposuction tube that *did* truly change me completely, but not the way I had intended.

I was in the holding area, pre-surgery, waiting to connect with my doctor before I was to start the whole "fix me" process once again. It was like I was watching a less-than-B-rated horror movie, where all the signs for the soon-to-arrive-catastrophe were being blatantly laid out for me. It was a "get ready, here it comes, so grab your partner's arm, curl down in your seat, and prepare to scream" moment.

I am on the table, and the whole craziness starts right after that red-haired, blue eye-shadowed biker nurse gives me the anesthesia. I am lying there, when all of a sudden, I hear two other nurses begin to argue about – believe it or not – which one is responsible for losing some other patient's chart. I'm thinking, "No… no… they can't be talking about that. Especially not right now! You've got to be kidding me. What's goin' on?" In that seemingly overstretched moment, I began to feel the results of the injection taking effect. Regretfully, I was becoming drowsier and weaker as time warped on – and as that twisted nurse conversation went on and on. It was so inappropriate, so ridiculous, and I'm sure it lasted for at least ten insane minutes, maybe even longer. Who's to say? With that kind of liquid juicing your system, what seemed to be ten minutes could just as well have been twenty minutes, or ten seconds for that matter.

I also started wondering, "Where is the doctor? He's late. I thought he was supposed to come and check up on me." Just then, I started to feel my chest go all cold inside, at the same time as I was feeling my feet starting to burn. My eyes felt like they were starting to twitch, and I was just thinking, "*Oh no*... please don't let all of this be signaling my Doomsday." Yes, darkness, shadows and looping lights began surrounding me. The nurse's outfits were contorting into prison uniforms. It was just crazy.

It was then that I began thinking, "Carlton, see... *you trying to suck out just a little more ugliness might be going too far.* Carlton you've seen the talk shows, you've heard the tragic stories people spew out after they've made some obviously stupid choices. *What are you doing?"* That's when the real panic thoughts rolled in. But by that point, I was way too weak to even lift up an arm, so there was no way for me to protest. The nurses were doing their thing, the doctor was nowhere to be found, and I was fading fast.

Then I remember that, like a bolt of lightning, God

came quickly into my consciousness. And I immediately started talking to him, and talkin' fast. "God," I was saying, "please, if you bring me out of this with no tragedy to my face, *I will never do this again.* I will make myself learn to love what I am. Please, God, don't let me go this way. I'm sorry. I will accept me as You made me."

That life-scare moment was ringing loudly in my head as I woke up in the recovery room, feeling nervous as hell. I began moving ever so slowly. Not because of the injected drug, but because I wanted to carefully monitor how all of me had adjusted to what had happened. Was I paralyzed from the chest down? Was I able to see properly? All of those twisted type of questions. Then I recall wanting to remain totally quiet – quiet until I could get home and see if my face had contorted into some *now-truly-disgraceful configuration.*

I can say, once I did make my way home, I did my usual mirror check and found there to be no complications at all… none. None! Yeah!!! Now, for as shallow as cosmetic surgery is thought to be, there was no levity about it coming from me. I was dead seriously Grateful with a capital G.

I remember I stayed there in my house, locked up, with no outside influences coming to me at all, for the next four days. This was not only to heal from the surgery, but also to work on healing myself from the mental baggage I had been carrying around. I learned from my Nip/Tuck experience that, whether self-deprecating thoughts are there for years, weeks or just mere seconds is irrelevant. That kind of thinking should *never* be going on inside of me.

That's how I was changed. Even today, some eight years later, with my face only marginally different from when I had even my first invasion, I am still growing into the new paradigm of accepting that Me Loving Me needs to be in order, no matter what perceptions may exist about my esthetic or qualities of character. Sometimes it takes much work, but that's okay. Life ain't for livin' scared. And that's just that.

Chased Down

"After that night when Gary and I were on the sofa bed, and his wife and baby were in the other room, I knew that I wasn't going to do what we had been doing anymore. I was feeling like, 'This is all just too wrong and now I get it.'

Then one day after that, I am in the dojo with Gary, and we finish our karate lesson. All the students leave, and now it is just Gary and me. I can tell he is going to want something to happen there. It's sort of the way he doesn't look at me that lets me know he is going to really be looking at me. He is putting things away, and it feels all just too much like business versus him looking at me warmly. I know what he has in mind.

It is about 7:30 in the evening, and the room has that sweaty smell because we have just worked out. Fluorescent lights always feel weird to me, and I remember the fluorescent lights in the gym, opposite the darkness coming from the store front window because it was getting late.

I don't remember how it all starts, if he comes up to me or what, but I seem to remember him sitting down. He starts off small, tries to keep it light, calls me over. By the time I get over to him, he has that look that he wants me to touch him. I don't want to. I remember him trying to make a move, me trying to stop it, and him getting aggressive.

I remember him grabbing my wrist. He pulls me closer. I say, 'Let go of me.'

I yank my hand away and he grabs me again. He has his hands around my waist as I'm trying to get away. I fall down. I'm down on the floor. He's starting to pull himself onto me, and in some very spastic way – as a thirteen year old fighting off a grown man – I'm letting him know that I need him to stop.

'I'm not into this. I don't want to do this anymore.'

I saw panic on his face for the first time, as he realized the stage he had gotten to with it all. And he stopped and immediately started apologizing, saying, 'I'm sorry. I don't want to do that to you.'

I was now absolutely clear that it was all fucked up, and he was fucked up, and I just wanted to go home.

I told him to take me home. And until I went back to Florida to confront him in 2006, I never saw Gary again after that day at the dojo when I was thirteen.

I don't remember details about that night, like changing out of my little karate outfit. Yes, by the time the five years of molestation finished, I was a brown belt in karate. How ironic.

After I fought Gary off, I don't remember anything – the ride home, if I cried when I got home, if I just went in and did my homework. Like I don't remember certain details about that day with the oranges out by the pool. I don't remember if we got up afterwards and ate something. I don't remember Tony waking up.

My memory bank is dead about certain things…

Even though my relationship with Gary was twisted, it was tricky for me. Because my

father relationship was so toxic, I never had a man in my life that was giving me any kind of meaningful validation. I was clearly not getting that at home. Not only was I not getting a lot of appreciation from my Dad or from my peers, I felt people thought I was stupid. From my Dad's voice, we were just Goddamn kids.

'One way or another,' I thought, 'I'm gonna get my validation.' And, when I was with Gary, that's exactly what I did.

So while yes, I was aware pretty much from the beginning that what I was doing with Gary was inappropriate, a side of me liked getting the attention. It was a big deal for me – getting a male authority figure making me feel like I mattered. There was a side of me that was reveling in that feeling. Our behavior did not become seriously wrong for me until that last year.

The first official gospel play I ever got to witness was in January of 2005 when I saw Tyler Perry's *Madea Goes To Jail.* The play had opened for its second sold out weekend in Los Angeles, and when I say that it was a truly, outrageously brilliant theater evening, I mean it from the fullness of my soul. Never, ever in my entire life have I had such a continuous in-shock, laugh-out-loud, wanna-take-my-shoe-off-and-throw-it-to-the-stage in admiration, entertainment experience.

Yes, the writing of the play, the performers, and the music all were very good, but it was mostly the wackiness of the lead character, Mabel "Madea" Simmons, played by Tyler Perry himself. From the very first moment that Tyler enters the stage as Madea, you just know he is going to have the audience in the palm of his hands, howling with laughter, for the course of the entire evening, with no plans ever of lightening up.

It begins with the way he ages Madea to be somewhere, I'm gonna say, close to seventy-five – and I'm not talking about a subdued, citified Diahann Carroll version of seventy-something. I'm talking about the more rural, matronly woman version. Like the endearing ones that might stand around, all testy-tempered, with sloppy, oversized, beige grandmother stockings banging all sweet and loose around their shins and ankles; and melon-sized water balloon breasts, flanked by jiggling arms surrounded by floral print polyester sleeves, held in a dropped elbow, wanna-be-boxer position, taking ridiculously wide-legged stances, fully stabilized for ass kicking, against the first person to step, in any way, out of line.

Then to the hilariously created moments of his saggy grandmother seducing the walls of her living room, then on the floor like a New York stripper, rolling around to the sounds of old school soul music, fantasizing about the young men she was going to work into a sexual frenzy.

All of that. Along with how he would, while keeping you thrust into laughter, even break out of his Madea character to break "the fourth wall," throwing ridiculing remarks to the latecomer audience members who were slinking their way to sit down, far too late. All of this was smoothly woven into such out-of-control brilliance. Yes, Mister Tyler Perry is a genius. And I am so thankful for his overflowing bucket of fun. So, for anyone that is ever even marginally close to one of this man's creations, you should run to see it, and run fast.

This production came to mind for me as I sat down to write this book, specifically because of how it linked to my own personal performing experience at The Kodak Theater, the same venue where Tyler's play was staged. I had been working there from September through December, 2004 in *The Ten Commandments* with Val Kilmer – an experience I can truly say I had only because *God chased me down* to give it to me.

You see, somewhere around the middle of May that year, I started getting phone calls from my agents with the idea of me actually auditioning for *The Ten*, as we called it. But I shut it down with a fast no, thinking it was beneath me, because they didn't seem to want to consider me for any lead roles. That was my response from the very first phone call. That was my decision, and I was stickin' to it.

A week and a bit later, to my surprise, the production called once more, requesting that I show up to prove my goods. They still had no thoughts for me as a principal, so my ego kicked in even further. I started in from this lofty place of, "Are they going to make up for my potentially measly ensemble role with more money? If they are coming back for me a second time, obviously they really want me, so we can use it as leverage. Blah. Blah. Blah." My agents then said that it was a "favored nations" offer, meaning that everyone in the ensemble would get the same compensation, with no negotiations to be had.

They also told me that the producers wanted people to *sing* for the audition. That's when the creeping feeling of fear took its place and the cookie started to crumble – I suppose because of the insecurities I had about my singing. My reps heard the frustration in my voice, and so they graciously followed suit with my desired "no" yet again.

Then, *I couldn't believe it,* about a week later, a third call from my agents came in regarding the Val Kilmer project. This time it was right around my birthday, so I used my special day as the excuse for why I couldn't go in. I said something like, "I'm taking the week off, and won't be accepting any calls regarding work." At that point my intimidation was rising so high that, if their numbers showed up on my caller ID at all, I didn't care what they might be calling me for, I would just decline to deal. The pressure of simply hearing them on the other line seemed to be just too much for me to handle. *This was a serious freak-out, about to go running rampant.*

Then my ego really starts raging, and I'm thinking to myself, "I could take some chorus part? Yeah? And what are they [the cast] going to think of me for doing such a small nothing of a role?" You see, I had actually stepped away from dance some twelve years prior in order to pursue my acting career. And while I did have some very strong years with acting, it was surely much more in a dry spell by this point – which was honestly the only reason I was even interested in dancing again at all. Yes, I wanted a principal position, but only on my disheveled terms. I was feeling way too *full of myself* – and it was only getting worse.

There I was in all of this, creating such insanity, while at the same time truly clinging to the hope of being loosed from my fear. So I decided I needed to call a good friend – Leslie – a dancer/actress/singer I've known for years. She is someone I have serious artistic respect for, and I followed her journey as she fully conquered her own singing intimidation thing. I got her on the phone and said straight out of the gate, "I'm having artist ability anxiety. Can you meet with me tonight and talk some sense into me?" Leslie had never heard such panic on my voice before, and so, like a true friend, thankfully, she said "Yes."

We met for dinner, and – you better believe – a couple of drinks, and I began to lay my heart on the table. By the end of it, she had convinced me that even though I had made *The Ten* production go away, I should start working with a voice coach immediately, not only to strengthen my voice, but to also build some audition songs for myself. That way, at least when other opportunities came up in the future, I would be more prepared and wouldn't have to feel so scrambled about.

That meeting was a Godsend, 'cause after our two hour fellowship, I was left feeling much more on track and was now really wanting to honor myself from a higher place. I mean, my voice never had been bad, but for whatever reason, I had bamboozled myself into an unnecessary mess. So, I decided, right then, that night, it was time for it to stop. And so, within about a week's time I contacted a coach Leslie had recommended and was well on my way; facing and dealing with my fear.

But those *Ten Commandments* people – they just would not let up. They actually reached out a fourth time. Now, I'm thinking, "*This is way too strange.* Something much bigger than what I'm focused on must be trying to happen here, 'cause Hollywood just does not behave like this." This time, I could feel the frustration in my agent's voice, and I knew I couldn't afford to piss them off too much, 'cause I needed them on my side. I had to be smart about things. I had spent the last couple of years taxing myself while working in seclusion in a restaurant – and I wanted out badly.

But let's back up to somewhere around late February of 2003. That year, I had actually begun reading the Bible, and was really beginning to feel the power and the real value of the Book. And the whole God thing. I had even reached the stage of praying to have God tracked through all areas of my life. This was a Carlton Wilborn way I had never known before. Then, by late April, I eagerly laid into reading a book I had heard about for a couple of years called *The Purpose Driven Life* by Rick Warren. It is Christian-focused, and is set up to help people get clear on not just their own desired path for life, but their path *through the eyes of God.* This God stuff was growing on me, and growing strong. So, thinking about all that was being revealed, this time I said "*Yes...* I'll go and prove my talents to these people." I was thinking *prove* my talents, God was saying *share.*

It was a Saturday audition appointment, scheduled as a very exclusive call. When I showed up, there were only about seven other performers (male and female) there. The casting people had us all dance first, then they sent us out into the hall, and had us wait while they debated about whatever it was they needed to go on about. It was such a trip. There I was, now actually feeling fairly calm and patient. I was just laughing at myself inside, as I hung in there, with my newly prepared audition song book. It was all neat in a binder, with my own actual "Carlton's Music Book" label on the cover. Oh, my actor tools were in full force now. I'm sure that for anyone that cared to noticed, it appeared that I had been doing this song-and-dance thing for years, which I had not. This was actually only the second musical I had ever gone up for throughout my entire twenty-year career.

So, I'm waiting and waiting. And the clock is ticking. Fifteen, then twenty, even thirty minutes pass before they start calling people in. I was the third person they smoothed into the room. I stepped into that audition box, holding my confidence tightly and praying the whole time that I wouldn't make a fool of myself. The accompanist did some dramatic shake thing to his hands – as if releasing the dust from his last victim. He lifted a delicate smile, nodded to me and then proceeded to play, and off I went. I sang a piece from *The Lion King*. It was the song "They Live in You." I chose it because it speaks about the spirits always being inside of you and always being armed to help you. As I sang, I just kept thinking about that message, and about God and what I knew he had gifted me to do – I needed whatever I could find to chill myself out. By the time the song finished, I found myself actually feeling that I had done a pretty damn solid job. I thanked everyone in the room, shook the hand of the pianist, then stepped out the door. And that was that. I had succeeded – at least against my scary monster.

Within only two days, my agents called to say that the producers wanted to offer me a position. No callbacks needed, but they needed to know within one day what I wanted to do – or else they were going to move on. Initially I thought, "How can they expect me to decide right away?" Then clarity immediately circled in and drew me to focus on all that had transpired, and all I had been praying about and for – which God had been trying all along to bring to me through *The Ten Commandments* – not only the artistic employment security, but the richer relationship with God through my artistic abilities. Once all of that registered, I then raced to the phone and said "Yes" to the job. At that point, I didn't care what they wanted to offer me, 'cause I was now knowing that God was trying to work something extra special out for me.

The Ten Commandments ended up being such a blessing for my life on so many levels. It brought not only the daily resonance of God and his Word to me, but that creative experience was putting in my face, on the regular, the tools I needed to understand more fully how I was to live my life

– from a character-quality point of view. Plus, it awakened me to truly begin to face my most pressing personal dilemma – my sexual demons. Yes, every night as we moved through the second act of the show, dealing with The Land of Milk and Honey section of the show, where Moses returns from the desert journey to chastise the Hebrews for being weak and giving in to their lust-luring idols, I would (while in full performance mode) be praying to be freed from the lusting bondage that had been weighing heavy on my soul.

The show then even provided me with artistic blessings that I did not expect – an original cast album recording (in which I had never before been involved), and a DVD, which was not part of the original contract. Both provided me with increased monetary blessings, allowing me to get a handle on some seriously long overdue financial issues. So, *yes...* gratitude for *The Ten Commandments* is something I was finally left with, no doubt. But even more grateful was I that God was watching over me to such a degree, *so much so as to stay right on my tail, chasing me straight into clarity.*

The major lesson I learned from that whole experience was that, if I am fully trusting in God, listening carefully to his rhythm and *his* will for my life, I will be blessed beyond what I could ever conceive of or do for myself. And I am committing myself to envelop this reality more and more.

I see that there are no challenges, there are only new configurations that we have to get comfortable maneuvering.

Thank you, God, for the lesson. *Thank you. Thank you.*

Thank you... for *The Ten*, and for The Ten Commandments. They've both done wonders for me.

The King That Is Me

Long after that night when I fought Gary off and finally put an end to the molestation, I was still saying yes to things I needed to be saying no to. And it all centered around me needing so much validation.

As an adult man, every time that I found myself with a partner, because I so wanted them to want me, I basically said yes to whatever their habits were – however destructive the effect might be on me.

The very first dude I really got connected to here in Los Angeles was Ken, who I mentioned earlier, who was way into drinking too much and taking pills, and so I began to drink like an alcoholic. I was able to stop easily after the relationship was over, but while it was going on, I was drinking way too much for my own good.

I met him at a bar in Silverlake. He seemed artistic. He was a sculptor and I think for me, having partners introduce me to worlds that were fresh and that I'd never experienced before was also part of the allure. Another good example of that was Mr. X – the trust fund baby, who could offer me all the doors that money can open.

Then I fell into my thing with the ex-stripper, who was addicted to porno and smoked too much weed. And then there was the ex-Wall Street stockbroker. We bought eighth bags of pot like toilet paper – as soon as it started to get low, we replenished. He was also into cocaine, ecstasy, acid and circuit parties... and though I had some curiosity, those harder recreational favors weren't really my thing. But of course I laid into it – pun intended – and took it all on.

The trap for me is longing desperately for them to want me – which gets me caught into all of this behavior that I know is not really for me.

All of this falls into the area of me following the voice and the path of the men in my

life – my perp, my Dad, and all the guys whose ugly behavior had a hold on me. Because I valued these guys so much, I valued their opinion of me more than I valued my own internal compass.

On a Saturday night, before I leave for Florida to go see Gary, I meet a man. We talk for maybe four minutes. He takes my number. Two days later he calls me, we do the usual this-is-who-I-am stuff for about forty-five minutes, and then we arrange to hang out the following night. He comes by my place, and within maybe thirty minutes of our meeting, tells me he needs to contact his brother about some sexual abuse his brother forced him into when he was a child. Ding, Ding, Ding… instantly my mind goes churning, like the fastest slot machine in the land.

I am shocked at his boldness in admitting to the same abuse I'd gone through. I believe I am being given a gift – someone who knows how to readily confess to being in the same predicament I was going through, someone able to offer the level of compassion I had so needed for so long. From there, we begin to merge. And merge. And merge even more.

I open up. I tell him I'm two months into a one-year celibacy commitment to myself. He makes no moves on me, seems to respect my position with absolute honor. He doesn't even make that same snide remark I'd heard from the two other guys I'd dated since becoming celibate. They had both said to me, "Yeah, dude… sure you'll last that long."

We really dig each other and we are not afraid. He goes so far as to tell me that he's never been with someone celibate, but will find a way to handle his sexual cravings when they arise. He tells me he'll drop the "booty call" guy he's been sleeping with.

I am stunned, delighted. I had never had a man showing me that level of respect. *With no sexual agenda attached.*

And then, like two kids, nervously thrilled to be plotting for some candy-inspired petty crime adventure, we begin to contemplate a monogamous commitment to each other. Yep, having spent a whopping four hours together, or five hours of knowing each other in total, we go with the "YES, let's do it" choice, and right then and there, become fully locked-and-loaded hitched. Red flag number one.

Then, within only seven days of my return from Florida, the toxicity rolled in.

"Why are you standing like that? Dude, take your hand off your hip. Are you sure you are cooking the food right? I don't like those clothes together. Oh, look at that frilly scarf." He was relentless in his dissecting of my every decision. And sure I was making my protests, but he just carried on in one fashion or another every single time we got together. There was no white light to be found. The second red flag.

Where was the king that I knew was inside of me?

How did I end up in a verbally abusive relationship right after returning from my life-changing visit to Florida? Me! The self-proclaimed iron man. The guy who walked around so proud, with his head so high? *It was all a ridiculous scenario from the get-go…and I knew it!* So, how had I let this happen? Why had I surrendered my no-sex rule? Why was I letting him talk to me like that, while I was making *us* breakfast, taking *us* to the movies, taking *us* out to dinner, because he didn't have enough money?

I agonized. I woke up at two in the morning, and three and four. I walked around the apartment. I turned on the television and watched my favorite preacher. I prayed, and agonized some more. I thought about the man who had taken so much from me, and the incredible journey that had brought us back together in white light. In the white light of forgiveness. And then I thought about this new man.

Then we end up in a bar – straw-to-the-camel's-back time – with us finishing a first round of drinks, and him telling me he was ordering another but that I needed to order water because he wasn't about to share his drink or spend any more money. I looked at him to see if he was smiling. No. No lightness in his tone. This was not a joke. The strange thing was that right before that ridiculous scenario, I'd stood before the mirror in the men's room, praying for God to give me an answer as to what I should do with him.

His behavior that night was the final red flag I needed to finally put an end to this already foolish game.

The first time around, I was a boy – too young to have a voice. The price for Gary's lovin' me was too high. And here I was again, being asked to let myself be loved by someone who abused me with his words every chance he could. The price tag was too high.

"Look, I don't care if you walk away thinking my take on this whole thing is wrong or too sensitive or whatever," I said. "I am not going to be treated like that ever again. I deserve to be with somebody that's honoring me, and celebrating all of who I am. I deserve to be with someone that helps my life be easier when I come home, not someone beating down my every move. I am *not* interested in being in some toxic relationship. I am not going to be abused any longer. I'm done!"

Those were words that my soul had never declared before, words that were essential to me moving beyond the past messes I had entangled myself in. White light was beginning to pierce its way through.

I see now that though the relationship was a challenge, and my drive to make sure we were going to last was ridiculous, it was also, yet again, a divinely orchestrated connection, set up for me to have the profound revelation of self-honor that I had awakened to.

That was the lesson this abusive man brought to me. Life was calling me to embrace the light, *and let the past be the faraway past.* More white light, that's what I was being beckoned toward. And that's where I was heading – towards the white light, shining brighter. At last, The King That I Am was standing stronger. Yes, from here on in, white light ever increasing, is what I intend to be about building, so that *The King That Is Me* will forever be expressed, recognized, and honored as such.

In a lot of ways, my life has seemed really sad. Yet, when I look at how much resilience got built up in me, curiously enough, I look at most of my past as a blessing.

Gary is who he is. What he's doing at this point in his life, I don't really know. My dad is who he is, and surprisingly, he has shown me more love today than I ever thought he was capable of giving.

That being said, all I know today is that from here on in, being happy or peaceful is my responsibility. It is about me being focused on what is or is not right for me.

Is it nice to get validation from other people, here and there, sometimes? Yes. But I am so grateful that I have finally arrived at a place where I can get validation, affection, and care from myself. And be responsible to myself.

Being nurtured is something that all of us need, but I have learned that it is my job to make sure that I am taken care of, and not to put that responsibility on anybody else.

If I want to feel and be acknowledged like *The King That Is Me*, then that is completely up to me.

It is my deepest prayer that in sharing my journey with you, that you might see a glimpse of yourself, and like I did, find the strength and hope that lies at the center of the King or Queen that is you.

May you always live your life front and center.

And may I never forget.

About the Author

Carlton Wilborn presents a powerful artistic and personal presence. A highly respected dancer and actor, his dynamic style and unique configurations of strength and artistry have kept him front and center on many stages of life for more than two decades.

Wilborn began his professional career as a principal dancer with the world renowned Hubbard Street Dance Company in Chicago. Blending street savvy and urban sensibilities with an inherent elegance and commitment to integrity, he naturally commands the stage. As a dancer, actor, and writer, he is a force to be reckoned with; and as a choreographer, director, and dance instructor, he guides the pursuits of fellow artists with the same level of excellence and creativity he brings to his own craft.

After working as a soloist for five consecutive years in Ruth Page's *Nutcracker*, and as a resident guest artist for nine months with Ballet Met, Carlton followed his internal compass to Hollywood. He quickly became one of the city's premiere dancers, landing the position of Madonna's pillar of strength for the *Blond Ambition* and *The Girlie Show* tours.

In addition to choreographing the upcoming motion picture release *Yellow*, starring Roselyn Sanchez, Carlton has appeared in over twenty film, TV and stage projects, including Madonna's documentary feature *Truth or Dare*, the upcoming Richard Gere movie *Hoax*, debut series *Lincoln Heights*; stage plays *Blade to the Heat* and *The Ten Commandments*; television shows *NYPD Blue, The Practice, CSI: Miami, L.A. Firefighters, Fame L.A., Oprah Winfrey Presents: Tuesdays with Morrie,* and *Made Men;* and commercials for Levi Strauss, Toyota, Round Table Pizza, Visa, Chrysler and AT&T.

Throughout his career, he has also worked with such entertainment luminaries as Herb Alpert, Natalie Cole, Janet Jackson and Michael Jackson; choreographer Twyla Tharp; legendary photographer Herb Ritts; Tony Award-winning director George C. Wolfe, and powerhouse producer Joel Silver, among many others.

Carlton has done charitable work over the years for Project Angel Food, St. Jude Children's Hospital and The Children's Hospital Los Angeles.

He recently formed his own production company, which is developing the feature film *Rising*, as well as its first television series *SiMo,* AKA *Sound in Movement.*

With his Treelife Publishing Company, Carlton is launching a library of inspiring and empowering books and CDs, the first of which is his autobiographically-based work "Front & Center – How I Learned to Live There."

Mr. Wilborn lives in Hollywood, California. His daily spiritual practices help keep his truth and principles always front and center in his heart, soul, and life.

AND NOW...

CHOCOLATE ICE CREAM AT 3:00.
EVERYBODY WELCOME.

ISBN: 978-0-9790052-1-3
51495
9 780979 005213

Printed in the United States
108820LV00002B/307-405/P